HOLINESS
for Ordinary People

HOLINESS
for Ordinary People

KEITH DRURY

Wesley Press
Marion, Indiana

HOLINESS FOR ORDINARY PEOPLE
Copyright © 1983 by The Wesley Press
P.O. Box 2000
Marion, Indiana 46952

FRANCIS ASBURY PRESS is an imprint of
Zondervan Publishing House
1415 Lake Drive, S.E.
Grand Rapids, Michigan 49506

Library of Congress Cataloging in Publication Data
Drury, Keith W.
   Holiness for ordinary people.

   Reprint. Originally published: Marion, Ind.: Wesley
Press, c1983.
   1. Holiness.   2. Sanctification.   I. Title.
BT767.D78   1987   234'.8   87-6141
ISBN 0-310-20731-2

Printed in the United States of America

90 91 92 93 94 / CH / 9 8 7 6 5 4 3

Dedicated to:
my Father
Leonard Drury
who lived a life of holiness
where it is hardest to . . .
at home.

CONTENTS

FOREWORD

Balance is an important ingredient in all of life. Issues, attitudes, and even life-styles are subject to being "overloaded" to the right or to the left. Dead center is usually tough to find. Even when we think we've discovered it, it's difficult to stay there. So it is with theology. So it is with the theology of holiness. Keith's book attempts to offer balanced teaching about biblical holiness.

Being an accurate imitator of God is dead-center holiness. Loving like Christ loves is perfectly balanced holiness. All of one's life is a God-given opportunity to pursue holiness. Oswald Chambers states well the human responsibility of holiness in the words, "my utmost for His highest."

It is difficult to fully and finally explain any intimate relationship. One grapples with terms and descriptions. Intimacy is impossible to put on paper in fully logical form. Holiness includes becoming very intimate with God. Discovering and delivering a theology of such devotion and intimacy with God is quite an art. Keith attempts to blend biblical doctrine and personal discovery in this book about holiness.

Some things I must understand before I can experience them. Some things I experience long before I have understanding of them. Holiness is to be both understood and experienced. And God keeps surprising us with expanding horizons of holiness in understanding and experience.

Keith Drury has written this book for ordinary Christians who are hungry for a well-balanced holiness – the extraordinary life.

David W. Holdren
Marion, Indiana

PREFACE

What comes to your mind when you hear the word "holiness"? Do you think, "That's for someone else, not me"? There is an ever-present tendency to relegate this important truth to powerful evangelists, saintly, gray-haired ladies, and dedicated missionaries. How unfortunate!

The work of entire sanctification and a walk in holiness is for every believer. Holiness must not be reserved for a select few of God's people who live above the ordinary humdrum of daily life. It must not be reserved for preachers, missionaries, and retired folk who "have enough time to pray all day." Holiness is for all of us. It is for ordinary people living an ordinary existence on this globe. Holiness is for factory workers, housewives, office managers, company executives, teachers, college students, and young married couples. This work of God is for all who desire a life of complete obedience to Christ. In short, holiness is for you.

The book is not a study of John Wesley's teaching (though anyone familiar with Wesley's writings will recognize frequent parallels). It is not a Bible study (though each chapter includes a Bible study section). It is not a scholarly study of the doctrine, though it is based on such studies of the past and present. This book attempts to present holiness in an understandable, life-related manner. It is written for all serious seekers after Christ, but especially with younger adults in mind. In a sense, the author has been a "translator" of the excellent scholarly works on holiness, placing these concepts in everyday language. He has attempted to outline a present-day "plain account" of holiness.

This book is presented with the prayerful hope that the reader will be drawn toward Christ, hungering and thirsting for a life of total obedience to our loving Master.

–K.W.D.

1

Sanctification Overview

Usually a book concludes with a summary chapter. This book is different. The summary of the basic concept of holiness and sanctification has been placed at the beginning of the book to aid the reader in seeing where the book is headed.

Q. What is holiness?

A. Holiness is loving God with all my heart, mind, soul, and strength, and loving my neighbor as myself. Simply put, holiness is Christlikeness. Holiness is, therefore, not really an "it." I need *Him*. In Him I find purity, power, and assurance. Jesus Christ himself is the best definition of holiness. He loved His Father and His neighbor perfectly – and that is what holiness is: perfect love.

Q. Isn't holiness only a *goal* for all Christians to pursue? Is it possible for a Christian actually to become perfect in love?

A. True, holiness is a goal, but it is an attainable goal. God commands us to be perfect – as He himself is perfect. Only a cruel father would demand that his children achieve an impossible goal and then refuse to help them. Likewise, our Heavenly Father does not command us to be perfect without providing the means to make us so.

Thus, holiness is radically optimistic – possibility thinking applied to spiritual growth. The idea of holiness marches into the midst of our pessimistic age proclaiming good news. You can become all you were meant to be. You really can love God with all of your heart, soul, mind, being, and strength. You can literally love your neighbor as you love yourself.

Certainly holiness is, or at least should be, the goal of every believer. But it is more than some unreal, far-off hope for humanity. It is an attainable, present-day experience. Sound impossible? With God, all things are possible. He commands us, "Be holy." Won't He also provide the means for our becoming what He has commanded us to be?

Q: How, then, do we become holy?

A: We become holy – Christlike – through sanctification. Sanctification is something done in us. It begins at conversion progresses as we grow in grace, leads us to the point of entire sanctification, and continues beyond that point. Sanctification is God's Spirit at work in my mind, soul, spirit, body – my entire life – changing and renewing my desires, thoughts, interests, attitudes, and behavior. Sanctification is how God transforms me into His Son's likeness. It is God's grace – His action – in my life. Given my cooperation, sanctification will change the erring sinner that I am into the likeness of His perfect Son. God commands me to be holy. But with His command, He offers the grace of sanctification which is His means of making me holy.

Q: When does this sanctification begin?

A: Sanctification begins the moment you accept Christ into your life. Sanctification is God's work of transforming you into Christlikeness. For most people the greatest leap toward Christlikeness occurs when they accept Jesus as Savior. This first great leap called "initial sanctification" occurs when we are saved. It is the beginning of God's continuing work in transforming us into the image of His Son.

Q: Does a person really need anything more than conversion?

A: Yes. God, who has begun a good work in us (initial sanctification), wants to bring it to completion. So He continues to perform His work of sanctification in us day by day. When we accepted Christ, the Holy Spirit helped us desire to be like Jesus. This new desire to be Christlike steadily draws us toward right thoughts, attitudes, values, associations, and activities.

But, all too soon, we discover that not all of our old desires

14

are gone. We find remaining in us a craving for some of the activities, thoughts, and attitudes of our old life.

Thus, we begin a struggle. Usually, we side with our new desire. We choose to speak or think the way Christ wants us to. But occasionally – perhaps often – we vote with our old desire and find ourselves saying, doing, or thinking something we know is displeasing to God. We are distressed; so we repent and promise God we'll "do better."

Progress during this time often is painfully slow. We may, at times, resist the Lord as often as we submit to Him. But, as we gradually yield areas of our life to Him, He moves in and we become overcomers, at least in that particular area of our life. When we examine large blocks of time, say a year or more, we see that gradual spiritual growth has occurred. There are many ups and downs in our lives. The downs may at times take us dangerously near our old life.

But the Holy Spirit helps us increasingly choose with our new nature in Christ. We have been dying to the deeds of the old life. However, we are periodically made painfully aware that something in our nature still causes us to veer off in rebellion to God. We may especially have difficulty with inward or secret problems like stubbornness, lustful thoughts, self-will, sinful anger, bitterness, and selfishness. Nevertheless, we grow closer to Christ and we can see progress, though much less than we would hope.

What is happening to us? We are experiencing "progressive sanctification" – God's daily work in our life, bringing our thoughts, values, attitudes, habits, and activities into conformity with Christ's example. Our leap toward Christlikeness at conversion, or initial sanctification, did not end our need to grow. Thus, every obedient believer will continue to experience a gradual work of progressive sanctification.

Q: Don't most ordinary Christians struggle like this all their lives?

A: Yes, many Christians do. Most believers – even many in "holiness churches" – seem content to be "ordinary" Christians. But the Bible clearly calls believers to more than an ordinary commitment. We are repeatedly called to a radical Christlikeness that is far above an ordinary Christian walk.

The Bible promises victory – even over the times of struggle with our old desires. It provides hope for our complete victory. The truth is that many Christians continue to struggle with mixed desires most of their lives. For this reason, the message of holiness is for "ordinary Christians." It is, to them, great news.

A person who continually consecrates areas of his life to God will grow in grace and will gradually gain victory over sin. He may, at first, wrestle valiantly with his old desires. Then, as he commits more and more to the Lord, he will find greater strength in suppressing the unchristlike desires. He may finally reach a point where he experiences periods of peace. It may seem to him that his old nature has been "smothered" to death. But then it rears its ugly head again, and he realizes he is still inclined to disobey. This is especially true when he fails to rely on Christ's power to overcome his old nature.

So, the Christian continues to grow closer to Jesus Christ as he cooperates with God, who performs "progressive sanctification" in him. Even though he is a "new creation" in Christ, he is still bewildered by occasional, or even frequent, inclinations from his old self, which are contrary to God's will. Many believers continue this war for years, or even until the end of their lives.

Wesleyan teaching does not deny the fact that a believer experiences this sanctifying process, perhaps for many years – or even a lifetime. But Scripture clearly asserts that this need not be the case. God can, with our cooperation and faith, shorten His work and accomplish in a moment what is usually the work of many years.

Q: Most Christians understand "initial sanctification" and "progressive sanctification." But what does it really mean to be "entirely sanctified"?

A: When a person becomes a Christian, he takes a giant leap toward Christlikeness. We call this initial sanctification." As he grows in grace, he gradually kills off the deeds of the old life, putting on the righteousness of Jesus Christ. We call this progressive sanctification. It is after this growth that he usually comes to a new point of decision.

What is this decision? The decision is whether or not to "go on." Now the Christian knows that God wants all of him – as a living sacrifice. No longer can he cast the Lord a tidbit of consecration now and then to satisfy His demands. He realizes God wants all of him – his thoughts, time, talents, future, money, associations, hopes, possessions, reputation, habits, likes, and actions – everything! God wants him totally – holding back no secret sin, prized possession, or reserved habit. God wants him to remove the "no trespassing" signs he has posted throughout his life that told God to stay out. God wants him to say, "You can have it all. I am, totally and entirely, Yours alone from now on."

He is sick of part-time victory. But now he has hope that there is actually power from God to completely overcome sin. He places all of himself in God's hands, making a complete consecration of his all to Jesus. He holds nothing back. This is called "entire consecration." He gives his all to the Lord and decides to obey all the guidance of the Holy Spirit. He commits himself, from now on, to instantly obey the promptings of the Holy Spirit, whatever the cost. He's willing to go anywhere, say anything, do whatever God wants, no matter what people think or what price he may have to pay. He is now 100% committed to Jesus Christ, his *Lord*. His daily prayer is, "Not my will, but Yours be done."

What does God do with this offering? He accepts it. Immediately! If someone is struggling endlessly for entire sanctification, it is not because he must persuade God to give him something God wishes to withhold. Rather, he is struggling with himself about giving all to God. God is in the business of accepting offerings consecrated to Him.

God, through His Holy Spirit, now moves into the very center of this person's life, and performs a major spiritual miracle. When he was saved, he received all of the Holy Spirit. But now the Holy Spirit gets all of him. The results are dramatic.

The Holy Spirit can move into all areas of this person's fully consecrated life. He is now unhindered by internal resistance. He is free to perform a radical, internal cleansing. The most noticeable result will generally be in the area of *desire* and *commitment*. He remembers how, before he was saved, his life was largely dominated by a desire to please himself and by sin. Then, he recalls how he struggled as a growing believer, with conflicting desires – sometimes wanting to obey, sometimes wanting to sin. He now discovers one dominating desire in his heart – to wholly please his Master. His consuming passion is to be holy, like Jesus Christ. He has a fresh hunger and thirst for holy living. His desire to disobey is gone. He wants nothing in his life but total obedience to his Lord. His

17

heart is filled with a new love for God and others. Since obedience springs from love, he wants only to obey his Master perfectly. He still faces temptation, but his will is already set – he is totally committed to obedience.

His performance may still be far less than perfect, but his commitment is completely magnetized toward Jesus Christ. Rebellion is gone.

He will now be used for God's work in new and more powerful ways. After all, God's plan isn't to bottle him up and place him on the shelf to be admired by others – a real live saint. God wants to use him. Entire sanctification is always for service. The path to sanctification always leads back to the world and God's work there. What is God's work in the world? It is bringing sinners to repentance and helping believers conform to His Son's image.Thus, any man or woman experiencing this work of God's grace increasingly pursues God's work: to win the lost and help believers mature.

In short, this man makes a total consecration of his all to the Lord. Then God, in cooperation with him, corrects his heart's desire so that it is now 100% directed toward perfect obedience. While he may still fall short in practice, his motive is saturated by loving intention. This is "entire sanctification."

Q: What happens if a person comes to this decision point and decides against going on?

A: The chance to choose will likely come again, but sometimes not for a long period. However, most people who have experienced entire sanctification have done so after a period of searching, thinking, and study of the matter. The decision point does not just drop out of the sky one day with a 15-minute expiration notice attached. Perhaps we would better term this a decision *period*. We usually face the decision about whether to go on or not during several weeks, months, or even a year. You are probably not in danger of rejecting the Spirit's calling by sundown today. There is usually still time to seek Him. But you dare not be casual about such an important matter!

Q: Does a believer who is entirely sanctified have any room for improvement?

A: By all means. We will continually be conformed to Christ's image every day we are on this earth, and perhaps throughout all eternity. Growth never stops. The notion that there is no growth after sanctification is false.

In fact, there should be *more* growth. If your heart is entirely full of a desire to please your Master, you will invariably grow more. Your pure desire will draw you closer and closer to the full measure and stature of Christ. We call this "continual sanctification." Is there progress after entire sanctification? You can count on it!

Q: If an entirely sanctified person has a desire to please only Christ, how would he or she ever be tempted again?

A: There is no state of grace which exempts a person from temptation. Satan tempts us through the world in which we live, or by tempting us to pervert our natural desires. Entire sanctification does not place a believer "out-of-bounds" to Satan. Jesus Christ himself was tempted in every point like we are, yet He withstood temptation and remained without sin.

The difference for the entirely sanctified person is that *his will is set* – he is totally committed to obedience, even during a lengthy time of temptation.

Q: If he can be tempted, is it possible for him to sin?

A: Yes, there is no level of spiritual maturity from which it is impossible to fall into sin. Consider these two statements:

(1) It is not possible to sin.
(2) It is possible not to sin.

The first is untrue. The second represents the optimistic possibility of biblical holiness. It is possible in this life to experience God's work in our heart to the extent that we do not purposefully disobey our Master – because we love Him so greatly.

Some ask, "How long can an entirely sanctified person go without sinning?" This is like the question, "How many angels can dance on the head of a pin?" or "How many sins does it take to send you to hell?" It misses the point. The point is that Jesus came to earth to deliver His people from their sin. God can provide the grace to enable a believer to be delivered from willful disobedience to his Lord and Master. When his heart is full of nothing but love for our Savior, this love prompts obedience. If we love Him, we will keep His commandments. We obey Him to the extent to which we love Him. If we can love Him perfectly, we can obey Him likewise.

But even a completely sanctified person can think, say, or do something against his own new nature. Though he is completely committed to please Christ, he may entertain some temptation so long that he falls into sin. What should he do if he falls into willful disobedience? He should treat the offense with serious repentance, confess it to the Lord, receive forgiveness, and fully commit himself to avoid that sin in the future. He should make restitution where appropriate and then return to living the life of entire sanctification. The proper response to any sin is always humble repentance and restitution, with a firm commitment to mend our way in the future.

It should be understood that we are dealing here with sin — strictly speaking; that is, sin as voluntary disobedience to what we know the Lord has commanded. It is "willful sin." We are not saying that an entirely sanctified person is free from all "falling short" of the perfect standard of Jesus Christ. No human being is consistently as perfect as Jesus Christ. An entirely sanctified man or woman will fall short of God's glory many times. Any breach in this perfect law of God creates the need for the atonement and must be confessed when it is recognized. Yet, if the believer's motive was one of pure love and devotion, such a breach is not charged to him as sin. This may seem to be straining a point, but it is a rather important one to those who say that an entirely sanctified person can be delivered from the possibility of sin. (What we mean by sin is willful disobedience to the Lord.)

An example may help. After several hours of hard work in his hot garden, a father glances up to see his two-year-old toddling toward him with a glass of water for his refreshment. The father takes it, examines the smudgy fingerprints on the glass, tastes it, and notes that the water is room temperature. But he also sees the eyes of his little son, who is gazing up at him in admiration and devotion. What will he do? Certainly he will gulp down the water and thank his little boy for "bringing Daddy that great glass of water." This boy has fallen far short of the perfect standard of refreshing drinks. But he has completely fulfilled the royal law of love. Because his imperfect deed sprang from a heart of love and devotion, the father considers him blameless.

Any falling short of the perfect standard of Christ requires God's grace and cleansing. But we do not call this sin if the motive is pure love. Much of the service offered to the Master falls far short of perfection. But, as He continues to teach His child perfection, our Heavenly Father looks down into his devoted eyes and, seeing the motive of his heart, pronounces his works blameless.

While it is possible for an entirely sanctified person to fall into sin, it is also possible for him to not commit willful sin. To a person gripped by a pattern of periodic disobedience, this seems like an impossible dream. But it is not. It is possible to live in continual and habitual obedience to Christ.

The real issue here is not, "Can an entirely sanctified person sin?" It is "Can an entirely sanctified person live above sin?" If he can, he should. Yes, he could sin, but he need not sin.

Q: What difference does entire sanctification make in the actual daily life of a believer?

A: As we have already pointed out, the biggest difference will be in the area of total commitment. His hunger and thirst for righteousness will be the dominant force in his life.

There will be a difference in his daily life also. This is particularly true of the areas where growth had been blocked by his own resistance to the Holy Spirit. He now opens the door wide to all areas of his life, and the Holy Spirit immediately moves to transform these into Christ's image. Often there is instant victory in some areas of long holdout.

However, in other areas of need the complete transformation may come gradually. Rather than resisting the Holy Spirit's entrance into new areas of his life, he is now "following after the Spirit" – adjusting, committing, recommitting, and submitting each area of his life as he is "led by the Spirit." Before, he struggled against both the Enemy and the Spirit. There was a war inside him. Now, he is fully allied with the Spirit in the war against the Evil One.

After this transformation, he will likely experience greater service to the Lord, particularly in the area of soul-winning. It may not occur immediately. But, before long, this believer will find himself drawn into some kind of soul-winning related endeavor.

Many experience new opportunities to help other believers grow in grace. People seem to "just happen to stop by" to talk about their own needs with him. This is natural. Since his life is dominated by the one Great Cause of living, it makes sense that he would be about his Father's business. The Heavenly Father's business on earth is evangelizing the lost and helping believers mature.

He will certainly see new victory over self-will, anger, pride, lustful thinking, materialism, selfishness, complacency, envy, jealousy, cruelty, lukewarmness, selfish ambition, and the like. Freedom that once sounded impossible is now experienced. He is at peace inside. The temptation to the above sins must recur but his inclination to do them is gone.

In place of the "garbage" of his old nature, he experiences a distinct increase in his patience, gentleness, kindness, happiness, contentment, satisfaction, meekness, self-control, joy, peacefulness, humility, sincerity, and, most of all, love. These attitudes and qualities have not come to the full perfection of Christ's example. But they have grown so much he feels he might burst. He has taken a giant leap in spiritual growth.

His hunger for further growth drives him forward. He becomes more sensitive to sin and temptation. He is more careful to avoid hurting others. He becomes teachable and is readily instructed or corrected when he is wrong. He is drawn deeper into the Word and prayer and establishes other habits that indicate his devotion to God.

He becomes increasingly active in caring for the poor, widowed, orphaned, jailed, or others in distress and need. He actually finds himself searching for opportunities to use his resources to aid others.

Of course, all of this does not happen at once. After all, this treasure is in a "clay pot." He continues to be human. But he has made a lot of spiritual progress in only a short time. He has experienced a "time warp" in his spiritual growth. He is a new person. His daily walk is quite different than before. Certainly, he still has much room for improvement. But his desire and commitment is 100% pure – to please Jesus. Even where he falls short in some way, it is because of human weakness and it is not by willful disobedience. He no longer must spend so much energy fighting his own evil desires. He now concentrates on acts of righteousness and mercy. He is radically different in his daily walk.

Q: Where can I find real live examples of this kind of life?

A: Spirit-filled Christians are all around you. Whom would you nominate as the person you know to be most full of love for God and others? You can probably think of several. In just about every church, of every denomination, in every

country, you can find people who have totally committed themselves to God and have been filled with perfect love.

Entirely sanctified people are not likely to brag about holiness. In fact, they may be embarrassed if you were to tell them
how holy you believe they are. But, when you think of the
lives of church people, several often immediately surface as
"obviously saints". Often, these saints may be older folk. However, it need not be so. A multitude of young adults and even
youth have been perfected in love. A great revival of holiness
is currently happening among this very age group. So don't
limit your search to the elderly, or to those who advertise their
holiness. But search among people living in the daily trenches
of life, who possess a pure love for their Master and a consis-
tent love for their fellowman. These have likely experienced
exactly what we have been talking about.

In fact, a person who possesses perfect love may not even
understand everything you have been reading in this book.
Many people misunderstand the doctrine, yet have experienced
its truth in life. Sad to say, there are also many who understand
the doctrine, yet have not experienced its reality in them. Understanding doctrine is important. But experiencing God's
grace in our life is more important.

Ordinary people are living the holy life. They are seldom,
if ever, in the majority, and they are not inclined to brag about
it. But in almost every church you can find some.

**Q: How can you know that you are indeed entirely
sanctified?**

A: First, I can examine *my heart's desire* – is it entirely
and completely magnetized toward Jesus Christ? Do I love God
with every bit of my heart, mind, soul, and strength? Is there
no mixture of desire in my heart? Have I nothing lingering
there making me want to disobey God?

Second, I can *examine my love for others.* Does my heart
well up with love for other people: those who are unfriendly
or unkind; the poor, helpless, and needy; those without Jesus
Christ; even those who consider themselves my enemies? Is
there any remaining bitterness, envy, jealousy, unforgiving
spirit, or wrath toward any other man or woman? Do I entirely
love others as much as I love and care for myself? These are
evidences of perfect love for others, which God creates in me.

Third, have I *totally consecrated my all to Jesus?* Is there
anything I have held back? Have I kept back some secret sin?

Have I placed a "no trespassing" sign to God in any area of my life? Does God have all of my time, talents, money, possessions, future, and family – every bit of me?

Fourth, have I experienced a *growth leap toward Christlikeness?* Was there a time when, after giving all, I experienced a major growth toward Christlikeness? Have I found the power to resist all willful sin?

Fifth, *has the Holy Spirit witnessed to me* – inside me – that He has performed this work? This witness may not have been clear at first, and it may become sometimes stronger or sometimes fainter, but do I know it is done?

All of these combine to give me enough evidence so that I can, with assurance, say God has indeed entirely sanctified me.

Q: Could you summarize the essentials of this experience of entire sanctification?

A: Yes. These 10 points include the most important ideas:

(1) Entire sanctification is perfect love – loving God with all my heart, mind, soul, and strength, and loving my neighbor as myself.

(2) Entire sanctification occurs after conversion. At conversion we are "initially sanctified," but we are urged to go on unto perfection.

(3) Entire sanctification need not be late in life. For many it may occur after many years, but it can occur much earlier.

(4) Entire sanctification is preceded by growth. This gradual death to sin and becoming alive to righteousness is called "progressive sanctification" and leads us into the experience of entire sanctification.

(5) Entire sanctification is followed by growth. In fact, growth toward the perfect standard of Jesus Christ will then be more vigorous.

(6) Entire sanctification is not absolute. We can be pure in motive and intention, but our performance may still frequently fall short of Christ's absolute standard of perfection. However, we can be delivered from purposeful disobedience to our Lord.

(7) Entire sanctification may be lost. There is no height of grace from which it is not possible to fall and finally be lost if we choose to do so. Yet, becoming finally lost is not such a likely danger that we must live in "eternal insecurity."

(8) Entire sanctification occurs instantaneously. Though it is preceded and followed by growth, there is a certain point when the old nature dies and the heart is full of nothing but a desire to please Christ fully.

(9) Entire sanctification requires our consecration and faith. If we will give our all to the Lord and reach out by faith, trusting Him to perform this work, He will do it.

(10) Entire sanctification results in a life of loving service. Its purpose is not to make us feel good, or to make us saintly monuments; but it is to make us clean vessels for our Master to use in His work of winning the lost and helping believers grow toward the image of His Son, Jesus Christ.

Are you a "seeker" after this kind of Christlikeness?

BIBLE STUDY

Use your own personal Bible for the studies at the end of each chapter in this book. If you are interested in making a serious study of the truth concerning this experience of entire sanctification, the Bible study section in each chapter will be of vital importance to you. Holiness is not a scheme some person dreamed up and then went to the Bible for proof. That we can be holy is clearly taught in the Scriptures.

You will find it especially helpful to mark the study scriptures with a red pencil as you go along.

With the overview information you now have regarding entire sanctification in mind, study each of the following scripture portions carefully. Then select the statement which best represents what you think to be the truth of that scripture.

MATCHING

—1 Peter 1:15,16

—2 Thessalonians 2:13

—2 Corinthians 7:1

—Romans 12:1

—1 Thessalonians 5:23-24

—Philippians 3:12-15

A. Sanctification begins the moment we are saved. It is our first growth leap toward Christlikeness, called "initial sanctification."

B. After we are saved, we must work with the Spirit at purifying ourselves – putting off sin and putting on righteousness. This is called "progressive sanctification."

C. God demands that we be holy in all of our life. In fact, He expects us to be holy as He himself is holy.

D. Our part in all of this is "consecration" – offering to God all of us.

E. Though an entirely sanctified person still falls short of perfect Christlikeness in his performance, he must still press on toward full Christlikeness.

F. God is able to sanctify us completely – our whole spirit, soul, and body.

For Review and Discussion

1. What is the simplest definition of holiness you can construct?

2. What is the difference between "holiness" and "sanctification"?

3. What is the difference between sanctification and entire sanctification?

4. In what ways does an entirely sanctified believer have room for improvement?

5. What two general definitions of sin do Christians use? Which one relates to the statement "You can live above sin"?

2

It's Everywhere

Holiness in the Scriptures

The idea of holiness is virtually everywhere in the Bible and in Christian history. It is not some new notion dreamed up by John Wesley or the "holiness churches." Holiness is taught clearly in the Old and New Testaments, and has continually been a concern for serious Christians through the ages.

The Idea of Holiness

Holiness originates with God. He alone is perfectly holy. His holiness is such an essential part of His nature that the prophet, Amos, declared He has "sworn by his holiness." All holiness begins with God. He is the Holy One.

> The sovereign Lord has sworn by his holiness. **Amos 4:2**

However, the idea of holiness in the Bible is not limited to God. Sometimes *places* were considered holy. On the occasion of Moses' encounter with God at the burning bush, he stood on "holy ground." There are *times* which were to be kept holy. The most obvious one was the seventh day of each week.

> "Do not come any closer," God said. "Take off your sandals, for the place where you are standing is holy ground." **Exodus 3:5**

> Remember the Sabbath day by keeping it holy. **Exodus 20:8**

Certain *objects* were considered holy; for instance, the altar, sacrifices, and related items used in temple worship. Even *people* could be considered holy, including priests, Levites, or even the entire nation of Israel. In fact, the idea of separation, purification, and holy living is a dominant theme of the entire Bible.

Holiness Promised

Throughout God's Word there is the dual promise of forgiveness for sins and deliverance from the power of sin. God's Word repeatedly emphasizes themes of individual cleansing from all impurity, renewing our hearts in righteousness, and conforming human beings to God's image.

In the New Testament, John the Baptist announced to those repenting of their sins that a greater One was coming who would baptize with the Holy Spirit and with fire, burning away all the "chaff" of men's hearts.

The hope for true deliverance from sin that would enable a believer to live in obedience to God's laws is found throughout God's Word.

The Standard of Holiness

Since God is a holy God, what does He expect from His followers? Nothing less than holiness. Moses prefaced the giving of various laws to the Israelites with the command that they be holy because God himself was holy. In the New Testament, Peter recalled this ideal by commanding Christians to be holy, since the God who called them was holy. Jesus concluded His demand to love even our enemies by stating that

Whatever touches any of the flesh will become holy.

Leviticus 6:27

I will sprinkle clean water on you, and you will be clean; I will cleanse you from all your impurities and from all your idols . . . I will save you from all your uncleanness.

Ezekiel 36:25,29

I baptize you with water for repentance. But after me will come one who is more powerful than I, whose sandals I am not fit to carry. He will baptize you with the Holy Spirit and with fire. His winnowing fork is in his hand, and he will clear his threshing floor, gathering the wheat into his barn and burning up the chaff with unquenchable fire.

Matthew 3:11,12

The Lord said to Moses, "Speak to the entire assembly of Israel and say to them: 'Be holy because I, the Lord your God, am holy.' "

Leviticus 19:1-2

But just as he who called you is holy, so be holy in all you do; for it is written: "Be holy, because I am holy."

1 Peter 1:15, 16

we should be perfect as our Heavenly Father is perfect.

The logic here is simple: (1) God is holy; (2) God called us to be like Him; (3) We must be holy, like Him.

What is this holiness that God expects of His people? It is obedience. God expected each Israelite to fear Him, obey Him, and serve Him with all his heart and soul. Obviously, this cannot be done with human strength. So God promises a work in the heart – a "circumcision of heart" – that can enable a follower to actually love God with all his heart and soul.

Solomon dedicated the new Temple in the presence of all Israel. He concluded his dedication by commanding them to fully commit their hearts to God. He warned them that God would not be satisfied with partial commitment; He demands total commitment. The record of the Israelites illustrates how infrequently they achieved complete obedience. But their failure has not altered God's standard of holiness. He wants total and complete commitment.

Jesus reinforced this high standard of holiness. He established it as the "most important commandment." Believers are commanded to love God with all their heart, soul, mind, and strength – their whole being; not with part of their being; not even with most of their being. Jesus commanded loving God with all our being. "ALL" means just that – 100%.

Then, just in case we are tempted to become holy recluses, Jesus attaches the second command: "Love your

> Be perfect, therefore, as your Heavenly Father is perfect.
> **Matthew 5:48**

> And now, O Israel, what does the Lord your God ask of you but to fear the Lord your God, to walk in all his ways, to love him, to serve the Lord God with all your heart and with all your soul.
> **Deuteronomy 10:12**

> The Lord your God will circumcise your hearts and the hearts of your descendants, so that you may love him with all your heart and with your soul, and live.
> **Deuteronomy 30:6**

> But your hearts must be fully committed to the Lord our God, to live by his decrees and obey his commands, as at this time.
> **1 Kings 8:61**

> The sovereign Lord has sworn by his holiness.
> **Amos 4:2**

> "The most important one," answered Jesus, "is this: 'Hear, O Israel, the Lord our God, the Lord is one. Love the Lord your God with all your heart and with all your soul and with all your

neighbor as yourself." These two commands – loving God and loving your neighbor – provide the clear standard of holiness commanded throughout the Bible. God is holy. He expects us to be holy. Holiness is loving devotion to God and others.

The most obvious command toward holiness is "be holy, because I am holy." Because we are God's, and He is holy, we, too, are commanded to be holy.

Jesus prayed, on His last night with His disciples, that His Father would sanctify them – His closing intercession for His disciples. This sanctification was for service – they were headed into a hostile world with a holy message. Jesus expected a future sanctifying work to be done in these followers which would equip them with the power and unity to work in an evil world.

All through the epistles the early believers are repeatedly urged to be filled with the Spirit, or to put on a new man, or to believe that God will sanctify them through and through. Paul wrote to his Christian brothers in Thessalonica that it is simply God's will that they be holy.

Holiness is clearly God's will for His followers. It always has been. It still is. It always will be.

Holiness Is for Believers

Some have been inclined to think that the commands to holiness in the Bible are not meant for believers. They reason that a Christian "gets it all at once." A serious reading of the Bible does not support this notion. Repeatedly the Bible writers urge Chris-

mind and with all your strength.' "
Mark 12:29-30

"The second is this: 'Love your neighbor as yourself.' "
Mark 12:31

But just as he who called you is holy, so be holy in all you do; for it is written: "Be holy, because I am holy."
1 Peter 1:15,16

"Sanctify them by the truth; your word is truth. As you have sent me into the world, I have sent them into the world. For them I sanctify myself, that they too may be truly sanctified."
John 17:17,18

Therefore do not be foolish, but understand what the Lord's will is. Do not get drunk on wine, which leads to debauchery. Instead, be filled with the Spirit.
Ephesians 5:17-18

It is God's will that you should be holy.
1 Thessalonians 4:3

Since we have these promises, dear friends, let us purify ourselves from everything that contaminates body and spirit, perfecting holiness out of reverence for God.
2 Corinthians 7:1

tian brothers and sisters to pursue holiness.

Paul tells the Corinthian "saints" to purify themselves of everything that contaminates either the body or the spirit in order to perfect holiness in their lives.

Paul reminds the "brothers" in Rome that their obligation is to the Spirit, not to their old, sinful nature. The deeds of their old nature are to be put to death.

John tells "children of God" who do not yet see what God is making of them, that they will be like Jesus when they see Him. This exciting hope is to cause these believers to purify themselves, just as He is pure.

Paul tells the Corinthian Christians that his prayer is for their perfection – that they will become whole, mature, and complete. He concludes with an admonition that they should aim for nothing less than – you guessed it – perfection.

In Hebrews the readers are scolded for being baby Christians so long. They are urged to leave the elementary teachings, and "go on" to maturity or completeness in Christ.

Finally, after detailing God's faithfulness throughout eleven chapters, Paul urges the Roman believers to present their bodies as living sacrifices, holy to God. He promises them a spiritual transformation or renewal of their minds, so that they will no longer be conformed to the patterns of this world.

There is no doubt about holiness being a clear emphasis of the Scriptures. In God's Word believers,

Therefore, brothers, we have an obligation – but it is not to the sinful nature, to live according to it. For if you live according to the sinful nature, you will die; but if by the Spirit you put to death the misdeeds of the body, you will live, because those who are led by the Spirit of God are the sons of God.

Romans 8:12-14

Dear friends, now we are children of God, and what we will be has not yet been made known. But we know that when he appears, we shall be like him, for we shall see him as he is. Everyone who has this hope in him purifies himself, just as he is pure.

1 John 3:2,3

We are glad whenever we are weak but you are strong; and our prayer is for your perfection.

2 Corinthians 3:9

Therefore let us leave the elementary teachings about Christ and go on to maturity, not laying again the foundation of repentance from acts that lead to death, and of faith in God.

Hebrews 6:1

Therefore, I urge you brothers in view of God's mercy, to offer your bodies as living

31

brothers, children of God, Christians, are repeatedly called to something more – to go on to holiness, full maturity, completeness, perfection.

The idea of holiness is everywhere in the Scripture. It appears in one form or another more than 600 times. It literally pervades both the Old and New Testament. The standard of holiness is clear: loving God with all my heart, mind, soul, and strength, and loving others as myself. It is not merely some distant goal we pursue with no hope of attaining. It is commanded as God's will for all believers. It is thus a present possibility for me to have a heart full of love for God and others.

> sacrifices, holy and pleasing to God – which is your spiritual worship. Do not conform any longer to the pattern of this world, but be transformed by the renewing of your mind. Then you will be able to test and approve what God's will is – his good, pleasing and perfect will.
> **Romans 12:1-2**

The Holiness Quest in History

Down through the ages serious Christians have thought, spoken, and written about holiness (perfect love for God and others) and sanctification (God's work in us which perfects this love). Holiness is not a new idea in recent history. There have always been people who took God's demand to "be holy" at face value. These people searched for a means of becoming as holy as God commanded.

The writings of early Christians, like Clement and Ignatius, ring with the hope for deliverance from sin in this life – to actually "walk as He walked."

Some early seekers of holiness figured they might find holiness through self-renunciation. These ascetics denied themselves comforts of life, isolated themselves from the world, practiced daily disciplines of righteousness, and became the long-lasting lay monastic movement. Monasticism is probably the most organized quest for holiness in history. The hope was that self-denial and spiritual discipline would produce holiness in this life. For many hundreds of years, the search for holiness and piety sometimes led to a monastery or convent. Despite the inadequacies and limitations of the monastic and mystical movements, the holiness which was to be found during these times was most often found in these movements.

During the early 1300's there were other examples of sincere piety like Eckart and other members of the "Brethren of the Common Life." In the late 1300's Thomas a' Kempis wrote his *Imitation of Christ*. He emphasized that personal holiness – a complete purity of intention – was possible in this life. Through this time there remained within the Roman Catholic Church a strata of faithful seekers after holiness through sanctification.

Like most reformers in the 1500's, Martin Luther provided no hope for deliverance from sin in this life. But some of Luther's contemporaries, notably Schwenkfeld and Munzer and a group called "Confessors in the Glory of Christ," emphasized the real possibility of holiness in this life.

In the 1600's Jeremy Taylor attempted to explain holiness as a practical possibility for the workaday world in his book *Holy Living and Holy Dying*. The emphasis began to swing closer to everyday living. Holiness could be for anybody who sought it, not just for those who dedicated their lives to hiding away in monasteries, seeking all of God.

George Fox, a contemporary of Taylor, was father of the Quaker movement. Fox not only refused to relegate holiness and piety to a monastery, but merged it with social concern and activism, as Wesley did one hundred years later.

During this same century (the 1600's) German pietism was fathered by Philipp Spener who proclaimed the necessity for holy living. He and his followers held small group meetings for Bible study, reading, prayer, fasting, sharing, and mutual edification.

In the 1700's the Moravians carried on the pietist concern for personal holiness. The Moravians' bravery in face of apparent death, during a stormy voyage to America, shook Wesley deeply and led him to continue the spiritual search that resulted in his conversion.

In the 1700's John and Charles Wesley preached, wrote books, composed hymns, sang, and debated; as did John Fletcher and Bishops Coke and Asbury, in America. The great Methodist movement which emerged emphasized the definite practical possibility of deliverance from willful sin and being filled with love for God and others. John Wesley's writings continue to provide a central reference point for today's "holiness people."

During the 1800's the doctrine and experience of holiness continued to ripple through most Christian movements and denominations. The Keswick movement was organized in 1874 to "promote scriptural holiness." Colleges and "holiness associations" sprang up as waves of the holiness "revival" spread further. Special "holiness camp meetings" were planned. Denominations were organized, including the Wesleyan Methodist connection (1843) and the Free Methodist Church (1860), and the Pilgrim Holiness Church and Church of the Nazarene (late 1800's).

In the 1900's the doctrine of holiness continued to spread, though not without some distractions and abuses. Methodism seemed to downplay this experience. In some holiness churches, "legalism" became a problem. "Special" associations or events for holiness promotion declined. In many places the holiness message became limited to the pulpits of the "holiness churches," the remaining holiness camps, and the work of certain scholars. Some holiness people gave greater attention to doctrinal purity than heart purity, resulting in a curious "creedal holiness."

In this last quarter of the 1900's there are clear signs of a new revival in holiness doctrine and experience. This new wave of holiness is especially apparent among the younger generation. They, like Wesley, are vitally concerned about merging personal piety with evangelistic and social concern. There is dramatic evidence of an increasing emphasis on holiness in Keswick and Calvinist para-church organizations and in the "mainline" denominations. Retreats are making a strong bid to be a new "special" means of promoting the experience of entire sanctification. Young adults, fed up with the hollowness of the lukewarm life, are beginning to search for something more. There are signs that we are on the verge of a widespread holiness revival.

We can say with certainty that the ideas of holiness and sanctification are not new. They are not merely "pet doctrines" of a few denominations. Holiness is rooted soundly in the Bible, has been sought throughout the ages of church history, and is now experiencing a revival around the world. There are always people who will read God's Word and see His demands clearly – to put off all sin, put on righteousness, be filled with the Spirit, and experience His complete cleansing from sinful inclinations. These honest believers simply assume that God would not command more than He would provide for. Since He commands holiness, He will provide the power for them to become holy. They believe God is able to make them holy in this life. Thus, they reach out in faith to God and consecrate themselves to Jesus. Christ's response today is the same as it has been all down through history. Those who hunger and thirst for righteousness – *He fills*. Those who become seekers – *will find*. Those who ask – *receive*.

BIBLE STUDY

In this chapter we observed scriptures from both the Old and New Testaments to illustrate the frequency of references in it to holiness. In fact, it may appear that we have been "proof-texting." However, attempting to see what the whole Bible says about one subject, is a sound approach for the serious student of Scripture.

Bible survey, though, is not the only worthwhile approach. Another method of studying the Bible is to work intensively on a small section, e.g., Romans 12:1-2. This is an exciting way to study, but we may tend to bring our own prejudices to these verses. In this kind of detailed study, we should, in fact, bring to bear on that small portion of scripture, the "whole Bible approach" mentioned above.

A third way to study an idea in the Bible is to take a large portion of scripture, say an entire book of the Bible, and see what it says. This has some of the advantages of the "whole Bible approach," yet the size is more manageable.

The following Bible study (and the one at the end of the next chapter) proceeds along the lines of this third method. Let's study the book of Ephesians and see what Paul says to these people about the Christian life and holiness.

1. What kind of people were these Ephesians?

   Ephesians 1:1

   Ephesians 1:13

   Ephesians 1:15

   Ephesians 2:1,5

   Ephesians 2:19

2. What does Paul urge these believers to "put off" in Ephesians 4:22?

3. What characteristics of the "old self" does Paul give?

Ephesians 4:25

Ephesians 4:26

Ephesians 4:28

Ephesians 4:29

Ephesians 4:31

Ephesians 5:3

Ephesians 5:4

4. What are these believers to "put on," according to Ephesians 4:24?

5. What are some characteristics of the "new self"?

Ephesians 4:2

Ephesians 5:1

Ephesians 5:2

Ephesians 5:4

6. What does Jesus Christ want to do with His church, according to Ephesians 5:25-27?

7. Paul urged the Ephesian Christians to put off the deeds of the old self, and to put on righteousness. The goal was to make them holy and blameless. In his prayer for these believers in Ephesians 3:14-21, Paul describes how he hopes they will actually become holy. According to this prayer, what is Paul saying?

Ephesians 3:16. The Ephesians were already strong believers. What does Paul ask God to do now?

Ephesians 3:16. Who is to do this strengthening?

Ephesians 3:17. What is the word in this verse that is the key to holy living?

Ephesians 3:18. What does Paul pray that they will have the power to grasp?

Ephesians 3:19. But grasping God's love is not even enough. What does Paul actually pray that these believers will experience?

Ephesians 3:20. Then, just in case we can't even imagine being completely filled with God's love, what does he say about God?

Ephesians 3:20. Where is the power to do this already at work?

8. In Ephesians 5:17-18, Paul commands these believers not to get drunk on – under the control of – wine. Instead what does he direct them to do?

To Think About
a. Since all believers already have the Holy Spirit (Romans 8:9), what does being filled with the Spirit mean?

b. When we say something is filled, how full is it? Does this bring any other verses to your mind?

c. Are there possible parallels between being drunk on wine and being filled with the Spirit?

For Review and Discussion
1. What Old Testament passages speak of holiness?
2. What is the standard of holiness in the Bible?
3. Who are some of the individuals and groups who are part of the holiness movement's "family tree"?

4. What is the common denominator among all these groups?
5. What are the similarities among these groups and today's movement?

3

Sidetracks from Holiness

Many doctrines of the church are abused, misunderstood, or taken to the extreme in one way or another. There is a "main line" for every doctrine. However, human beings have a tendency to take some good truth and ride off into extremism. Doctrinal emphases frequently become sidetracked.

This chapter traces some of the sidetracks from true biblical holiness. It is not done with any intention to be negative or critical of any person or group, past or present. Rather, the purpose is to offer the reader a helpful description of what we are NOT talking about when we speak of holiness in the remaining chapters. Every generation has had its holiness sidetracks. These are some of the more common ones.

Legalism
Some holiness people left the main track and took the tangent of legalism. They came to identify holiness with certain selected "standards." In the most radical manifestations, submission to a lengthy list of taboos was considered to be sound evidence of true holiness. These unwritten rules often dealt with hair and hem-length, jewelry, makeup, and colorful or extravagant clothing. The list also included a variety of forbid-

den activities commonly considered worldly.

Many of these standards were for women and especially related to avoiding tempting men toward impure thoughts. In some groups it became commonly agreed that these standards were "the outward sign of the inward work." Such legalism can easily be a sidetrack from the sound truth of entire consecration.

The trail of how this legalism happens is intriguing. The sidetrack does not happen until step 4. It goes something like this:

1. Entire sanctification requires a total and complete consecration of my all – I must be willing to sacrifice anything to God.

2. God often focuses on one or two of my problem areas in making His total claim on my life. These one or two areas of holdout become the test of my willingness to say, "Not my will, but Yours." If I am unwilling to submit to whatever God wants in these areas, I am not entirely consecrated, thus not ready to receive entire sanctification.

3. When I do totally surrender all to Jesus – even those secret areas of holdout – He does respond with a sanctifying work in me.

4. (Here is where the trouble begins.) I may therefore assume that these two areas must be the universal "price" of entire sanctification. Thus, because an individual ties entire sanctification to specific "things," they make their area of obedience the standard for everybody.

It is equally interesting to see how entire groups (congregations, areas, or even denominations) adopt certain taboos as outward signs of holiness:

1. At some point a person testifies, "When I finally gave up X and Y (you pick what X or Y is), the Lord fully sanctified me."

2. Another (still "guilty" of X or Y) says, "That's absurd – I'll never give up X or Y – not even to be entirely sanctified." Thus, he sets up his own test of submission. X and Y become more important to him than being holy. He continues to do X or Y, but he recognizes that he lacks power; his heart is not right. His problem is not necessarily X or Y – it is his rebellious attitude.

3. Finally, sick of his inward disobedience, he or she says to God, "You can have all of me – my will is in total submission

to yours — even if I have to give up X and Y." God cleanses him and he experiences victory.

4. (Here comes trouble again.) He now shares with his friends, "I refused to sacrifice X and Y. For years I said I'd never give those up. When I finally did, the Lord entirely sanctified me."

5. Soon this group is filled with people who faced the same "test issue" for their willingness to do whatever God desired. The whole group comes to accept that a person can't be entirely sanctified if they are wearing or doing X or Y!

6. The whole thing calcifies into legalism when these outward "test issues" are considered to be proof of the inward work.

God requires entire consecration — willingness to submit to God in all areas of our lives. However, we can't set up our own tests of submission. If a whole group does this in concert, they are in danger of legalism.

Legalism becomes a problem when I impose my own "convictions" on others. Though often done innocently, the consequences can be serious.

The greatest negative consequence is that legalism frequently becomes a stumbling block to others seeking holiness. They stumble over the false tests set up by "more mature Christians." We must always trust the Holy Spirit to do His convicting work in the lives of believers. The Spirit will point out to each individual areas of holdback.

A delayed consequence of legalism is what happens to the next generation. History is replete with illustrations that the following generation will either be lost from the kingdom altogether, or will reject all corporate standards of behavior, heading off on the opposite tangent of "anything goes." This tangent is at least as dangerous as legalism. Both are sidetracks.

God does require a total consecration — a willingness to be, say, or do all that He desires of me. But, what He specifically requires of me, He may not require of you. We can trust the Holy Spirit to faithfully convince each believer in a personal way. Insisting that my convictions must become yours is one pathway to the sidetrack of legalism.

Emotionalism

In college I worked for a building contractor who did some construction on a "holiness campground." The camp featured a large pavilion complete with a floor-covering of woodshavings. During my first day on the job, a young laborer asked, "What do they do in that big building over there?" A swarthy old carpenter immediately replied, "Well, Peter, that there is a holy roller tabernacle. You see, them holy rollers get in there and roll all around in those shavings 'til they come out of there lookin' like shaggy dogs. Haven't you ever seen people 'get blessed', Pete?"

I had attended that particular camp meeting for seven years and had never seen anything so startling or entertaining! In fact, the meetings could have had a bit more enthusiasm, in my opinion. But the old carpenter was sure that holiness was somehow connected with holy rolling.

Where does this misconception come from?

All down through history there have regularly been a variety of emotional manifestations when the Holy Spirit does a special work among His saints.

John Wesley was distraught about such an emotional sidetrack in 1762. He decried the outbreak of "enthusiasm" among a holiness group in London who went off the deep end, supposing they would never die, assuming they would never again be tempted, or feel pain, claiming gifts of prophecy or discerning of spirits, all amid "much noise and confusion." This outbreak of emotionalism brought a flood of reproach on Wesley and the doctrine of holiness.

Through history there has been a variety of emotional manifestations related in one way or another to entire sanctification, the filling of the Spirit, and holiness. There has, at various times, been quaking (hence, the "Quakers"), shaking ("Shakers"), "shouting," "running the aisles," being "slain in the Spirit," "getting blessed," and "holy parades." At least one fellow built quite a reputation for running at full speed all over the church on the tops of the pews!

How did this kind of emotional exuberance become identified with holiness? Easy. People *do* respond emotionally to God's work in their lives. The joy, peace, love, happiness, and enthusiasm are great. It is natural that humans express this joy in some way.

How emotion is expressed differs from person to person, group to group, and has changed in different periods of history. But an emotional response to God's work, especially His purifying work, is natural. People generally express this gratitude and praise to the Lord in socially acceptable ways. Each group has its unwritten standards of what is an "acceptable way" to praise the Lord. Each individual has his own limits, largely established by his background, reaction to his background, or temperament. The emotional expression may be quiet tears, a raised hand, two raised hands, a smile, a soft "Thank You, Lord," a "testimony," a boisterous "'Hallelujah," a shout, "applause for Jesus," or other distinctly individual expressions.

The point is this: people will always respond emotionally to deeply moving experiences – including religious ones. But they generally respond in a way that comes naturally to their temperament (more on this in chapter 10) and what is socially accepted or expected.

Emotionalism can be misleading. It is an appealing sidetrack from the main truth of holiness. The emotionalism sideline sometimes gets people seeking a "Spiritual Mountain Dew" to "tickle their innards." Emotionalism can be whipped up by preaching, song evangelists, or musical groups, giving a false sense of God's blessing when it is nothing but froth. Sometimes emotionalism can be a false indication of spiritual truth or maturity. Those who focus on mystical experiences are inclined to extend their own particular emotional response to others, expecting all who "really have it" to act like them.

Finally, like legalism, emotionalism can have grave effects on the next generation. Sometimes the children of those living in an era of emotionalism shift their gears in reverse and exclude all emotion from their religious experience. To them "respectability" is foremost, and all meetings must be held "decently and in order." They reject any pull at emotions and consider those who respond outwardly as "shallow," "baby Christians," or "interested only in froth."

This may be one reason why a large segment of the current holiness movement has so soundly rejected the practice of tongues speaking – they acutely recall what they felt were abuses of overt emotionalism in their own past and fear any return. (There are, however, other good reasons to question an emphasis on this practice.)

Men and women are emotional beings. We do not want a relationship with God without emotion any more than we would be satisfied with a marriage without emotion. But we can ride off on a tangent until the manifestations of our emotions take center stage. Jesus, not some emotional ecstasy, must always be at the center stage of holiness.

"Now-ism"

Some have spun off on the tangent of "now-ism." They have insisted that the options are clear: (a) holiness, or (b) hell. Their logic goes like this:

1. God wants me to be holy.

2. If I am not now holy, it is because I am resisting God's will for my life.

3. Resistance to God's will is willful disobedience – sin.

4. Willful sin leads to a broken relationship with God.

5. Therefore, I must become holy now, or go to hell.

The "holiness or hell" proponents have taken a good idea and run down a sidetrack with it. True, continued resistance to the Spirit's demands will bring serious consequences to a believer's relationship with God. But there is also a danger of pushing others into a hasty "consecration" which may become a substitute for true and entire sanctification. Believers have been pressured into claiming a work not yet received, just to escape hell. Some sincere seekers may simply give up when the promised deliverance does not happen immediately upon their cry for holiness.

A worse outcome of the holiness or hell notion is what happens to those raised under its influence. As often is the case, they return to the main track and promptly head off the opposite direction – into "optionalism." They make holiness "possible, but unlikely" for believers, reserving the experience for a select elite of God's children. They don't talk about holiness, read about it, testify to cleansing, or preach about its possibility. And, if they do, they never call it "holiness" or "entire sanctification."

The middle ground is:

1. God does want me to be holy – to love and obey Him perfectly.

2. To be holy is possible in this life.

3. I should seek to become holy – now.

4. Continued resistance to God's will can result in a loss of relationship with Christ.

5. But, as long as I am hungering for righteousness – walking in the light given to me – I am not headed for hell.

God does not threaten His children, "Be holy . . . or else." Instead, like a Father, He takes us by the hand and leads us toward the perfect image of His Son. He does not scare us into holiness, but calls us forward to complete commitment and cleansing. Our job: obedience. If we are walking in obedience to Him, He is anxious to do everything possible to help us grow more like Christ.

"Two-Trip-ism"

For some, holiness has been watered down to a mere "second trip to the altar." People testify to being "saved and sanctified" referring to two "events" in their Christian life. Entire sanctification is truly an epochal event. But to speak only of that event is a sidetrack from the main line. Holiness is predominantly a daily walk with Christ – "walking as He walked." When sanctification is treated merely as a one-time event, we depart from the scriptural idea of God's work.

Combining "two-tripism" with "now-ism" has caused many serious saints to dutifully take their second trip to the altar. This way lulls them into a false sense that they now "have all they ever need." Not true. Yes, there is an "event" side to entire sanctification – a specific time when we make a total consecration, and in faith accept God's cleansing. But sanctification is more than a crisis event.

Take marriage, for example. Certainly "the event" of marriage – the wedding – was an important crisis to me. I stood before witnesses and publicly proclaimed I was forsaking all others and taking Sharon to be my wife. Our wedding was important – we have a whole bookful of pictures about it. But our wedding did not make our marriage. Our marriage is a life lived together in light of our wedding commitment. Our wedding event initiated a rich, growing life of marriage.

So it is with entire sanctification. The event is monumental. But holiness is a living out of the covenant consecration we made to God at one point. It is as present and fresh as my last thought, word, deed, or motive.

Holiness Creedalism

A few have gone off on the tangent of "holiness creedalism." They emphasize "understanding" and "accepting" correct holiness doctrine, more than experiencing complete sanctification. "Protecting our heritage" may become a fetish with them, and they are fastidious about "checking out what these new people believe about holiness." They may jealously claim they belong to the only true holiness group and may reject as heresy any thought which disagrees with their firm position.

Holiness creedalism sets in when a person discovers that his daily life does not measure up to his beliefs. His head is right, but his heart is not. His first inclination is to become a seeker, "going on" toward what he believes in or once had. But that would require confessing need, something pride keeps him from doing.

The second option is to dwell on the "head knowledge" side of holiness, engaging in preserving the doctrine, hairsplitting debates, technical studies, and checking out others' beliefs on the subject. Such a person will seldom talk about his daily walk in holiness. He avoids descriptions of inner sin like pride, envy, jealousy, impure thoughts, selfish ambition, bitterness, holding grudges, malice, sinful anger, materialism, and self-will. He knows, too well, that his heart is generously endowed with some of these. He becomes more concerned with doctrinal purity than heart purity.

This is not to say that doctrine is unimportant – this book is, after all, one of the series of doctrinal books! Creeds, articles of religion, and doctrinal statements are extremely helpful in guiding us, and they generally flavor our religious experience. After all, we seldom receive unless we believe.

However, our concern must not be only for delineating a position on God's sanctifying work – but also for bringing people into this life of obedience.

Pietism

A few have left the main track and retreated into "pietism." They emphasize prayer, Bible reading, total separation from worldliness, fasting, and other disciplines of the spiritual life. Like those who fled to medieval monasteries, they place the highest stakes on being separate – "set apart" from the world. The world doesn't touch them. They don't touch the world.

The work of entire sanctification has two sides to it: purity from sinful attitudes and inner evil inclinations, and power for evangelism and ministry to others. Those on the pietism sidetrack focus only on the cleansing side. Thus, they become morbidly introspective, withdrawing from a needy world and boasting that their group is "small, but pure."

However, there are others who ride off in the opposite direction – to the power side. These emphasize only the infilling of the Holy Spirit and new power for witnessing and service, downplaying any purity from inner sinfulness.

Both, of course, are sidetracks. Holiness is a two-sided coin: one side is *purity* from sin, the other is *power* for service. God does not want His people to retreat into cloisters of perfection. Neither does He want His people to invade a needy world while ignoring the sinfulness of their own hearts.

The Main Track

The main track of holiness keeps Christ as the central focus of holiness. *Holiness is Christlikeness.* It is not primarily what you don't do or what you abstain from wearing. It is not some special emotional feeling. It is not a second trip to the altar to escape hell. It is more than a statement of doctrine, and it is not fleeing all contact with the world. It is Christlikeness. As long as Jesus Christ is the central thrust of holiness teaching, His "gravitational pull" will keep us from flying off on a tangent.

BIBLE STUDY

All doctrines have sidetracks. Most of the people who travel off on them are well intentioned. You may be tempted to say, "So many people mess up this business of holiness, how can I ever figure it out?" Remember that these sidetracks have taken centuries to develop. Some are quite well worn. To avoid sidetracks you need to stick to the Word and keep Christ in the center of your spiritual focus.

Holiness is clearly taught in God's Word. The Bible is our primary source for learning about holiness. Enjoy the following Bible study in 1 Thessalonians.

1. What kind of people were the Thessalonians?

1 Thessalonians 1:3

1 Thessalonians 1:4

1 Thessalonians 1:6

1 Thessalonians 1:7

1 Thessalonians 1:8

2. Would you say that there is evidence that they were already believers?

3. What does Paul then tell these people?

1 Thessalonians 4:1

1 Thessalonians 4:3

1 Thessalonians 4:7

4. Paul concludes the book of 1 Thessalonians 5:23-24 with a prayerful promise. What is he talking about here?

a. What does he want to happen to the Thessalonian people?

b. How extensive is this sanctification to be? How far should it go?

c. What does it mean to be "blameless"?

d. Who does Paul believe will do this work?

e. How certain is Paul that it can actually be done?

For Review and Discussion
1. Why do you think some have gotten sidetracked in their holiness teaching?
2. Most sidetracks are a result of taking a good truth or idea to extreme. What are the sound truths taken to extreme in each sidetrack in this chapter?
3. Some sidetracks are a reaction to other errors. List several sidetracks and their corresponding reactionary sidetracks.
4. To which sidetrack are you most vulnerable? Your local church? Your denomination?
5. What are the best deterrents to going off on a "holiness sidetrack"?

4

Images of Sanctification

Jesus frequently used images and illustrations to communicate truth to His listeners. He was comfortable illustrating a heavenly meaning with earthly illustrations. He used parables, metaphors, similes, and even an occasional allegory.

He found examples from His homelife. He illustrated spiritual truths with the leaven in bread dough, sewing patches on old clothing, and storing new wine in old wineskins. He moved into the world of nature, commerce, and interpersonal relationships with equal ease. He told stories about farmers sowing seeds, pearl merchants traveling all over the world, and a gripping tale of two boys in rebellion – one who ran away, the other who stayed home.

Why did Jesus use illustrations, images, and stories to communicate truth? Why didn't He merely list out what He wanted His followers to do and leave it at that? Jesus never wrote a book; He was a preacher. He preached to crowds on grassy hillsides, along roadways, and even in the midst of the noisy bustle of the Temple area. His listeners had no cassette recorders. They couldn't send for a printed copy of Jesus' latest message. They had to remember what He said.

Jesus was an effective communicator. He knew instinctively what most of us need to learn – people remember stories and illustrations best. Images give us a handle on truth. They penetrate deep into our hearts and minds, reminding us of the truth they portrayed long after we hear them.

However, there are limits in using images and illustrations. Most illustrations have one central truth. Yes, we may discover a wealth of other truths in a story, but these must be carefully considered in light of all scriptural teaching.

As we think about a few images and illustrations of sanctification, keep this in mind. Be careful not to go off the deep end, taking these illustrations as allegories and forcing every aspect to mean something. If taken too far, all illustrations eventually break down. If we stick to the central point of the illustration, these will be extremely helpful in understanding aspects of God's sanctifying work.

"Sacrifice – Who, Me?"

What does God want from His followers? Isn't accepting Christ enough? St. Paul, calling his readers "brothers" (Romans 12:1-2), urges them to offer their bodies as "living sacrifices" to God. What did this mean to his readers?

The ancients were familiar with rituals of sacrifice. Almost every religion had some form of sacrificial worship. In our day of humane societies and "I-brake-for-animals" bumper stickers, the whole idea seems odd and unusual. The Jews had a particular system of sacrificial rituals. Many chapters of the Old Testament are devoted to the exacting methodology prescribed for selecting and sacrificing a lamb, goat, or bull to God. The sacrifice was to be "perfect" – without any spot or blemish. This was to ensure that individuals did not bring their second best to God. These animals were offered as sacrifices for the sins of the people.

The Roman readers of Paul's letter would recall the Jewish sacrificial system when urged to "offer your bodies as living sacrifices to God." Did Paul mean they were to actually climb up on an altar and commit sacrificial suicide? No, he used the term "living sacrifice."

Paul was urging his readers to totally surrender to God. He used the illustration of a man bringing the best of his flock, totally surrendering it to God as an image of what the believer should do with himself. It is a figure of total consecration. We are to place our "all on the altar" – giving God our time, talents, thoughts, money, reputation, secret areas we are holding back, future – everything!

What will God do in response to total consecration? He will "renew your mind" so it is literally transformed. Then you will have the desire and power to cease being conformed to this world.

In summary, one aspect of the work of entire sanctification is the part we do – consecration. Before God will do His total and perfecting work in our hearts and minds, we must be willing to sacrifice anything – everything to Him. God doesn't want our second best or leftovers. He wants all of us – so He can use us to influence the lives of others. This is not a physical dying. Rather, it is the death of self-centeredness. It is sacrificing our inclination to be our own boss, being willing for the Spirit to lead us in all areas of our lives. Total consecration is offering ourselves as living sacrifices to God.

"Crucify Him!"

Crucifixion was a common mode of execution during Bible times. Compared with today's standards all forms of executions in ancient days appear "cruel and unusual." Criminals would be hastily tried, found guilty, and whisked off to their execution in a matter of hours. The crucifixion of Jesus is such an example of swift "justice."

The readers of the epistles were not strangers to the idea of killing. Their society teemed with violent executions, sometimes a thousand at one time! They knew what it meant to "crucify," "mortify," or otherwise kill someone or something. The New Testament writers continually speak to these people of the "crucifixion" of the old self, or "putting to death" what belonged to their earthly natures. (Read Romans 6:6; 8:13; Colossians 3:5.)

Crucifixion and execution repeatedly are identified with sanctification. Who or what gets crucified? – the deeds of the old life – the acts of the sinful nature. Bible writers frequently list a variety of examples of the old life's deeds, then summarily command believers to kill (do away with) them.

"A Good Scrubbing"

The first two images, or illustrations, help us understand our part – consecration – in sanctification. The next two images will help us understand better God's part in sanctification – cleansing and filling.

Paul uses the "scrubbing" image in connection with sanctification in his letter to the Ephesian believers (Ephesians 5:25-27). In the middle of a discussion on how a husband should treat his wife, Paul uses Christ's cleansing work as an illustration. This is, in fact, a triple illustration! First, there was the Old Testament sacrificial lamb getting scrubbed up for presentation to God. Second, there was Jesus who loved us so much He became our Sacrificial Lamb. Finally, there is God's cleansing work in us as individuals.

We will lay aside, for a moment, the truth to husbands here and notice Christ's sanctifying work in His church. It says:

1. Christ gave himself for us.
2. His purpose is our cleansing.
3. He does this by the "washing with water through the word."
4. He plans to present us to himself.
5. We will be radiant, without stain, or any other blemish, holy, blameless.

Do you remember the image of the sacrificial lambs we talked about earlier? These sacrificial lambs arrived in Jerusalem matted with the dust and dirt of desert travel. They entered through a special "Sheep Gate" and were taken immediately to a pool of water. At this pool they were thoroughly scrubbed until they were spotless. Only then were they routed into the Temple proper for presentation to the Lord in sacrifice.

What a striking illustration of Christ's work in us sanctifying, purifying, cleansing, making us holy! His sacrifice on the cross extends far beyond our conversion. Through Him we can be completely cleansed to be presented holy and without stain. That is what God does in purifying our hearts in entire sanctification.

"Spiritual Intoxication?"

You may have noticed, in your study following chapter 2 that in Ephesians 5:18 Paul selects a rather unique image to illustrate being filled with the Holy Spirit. He cautioned the Ephesian believers against becoming drunk with wine and encouraged them, instead, to be filled with the Spirit.

Is the use of drunkenness in connection with another kind

of filling accidental? I don't think so. People in all cultures understand drunkenness. Everyone has seen men and women who have "sold out" to alcohol. Alcohol becomes the driving force of their lives – coming ahead of their family, friends, job, wealth, position, power, or popularity. They are "driven to drink." Their thirst seems unquenchable. They are not satisfied with a mere "social drink." They are filled with one great passion in life – the "next drink."

When an alcoholic becomes filled with drink, he behaves in a totally different manner. He does things he would not normally even consider doing. We say he is "under the influence" of alcohol.

The image is dramatic. Substitute "Holy Spirit" for alcohol, and you have a description of a Spirit-filled man or woman. After I pledge my all to Christ, totally rejecting the deeds of the old life, He responds with cleansing and filling. When every area of my life is open to His workings, and I am in total submission to the Lord, His Spirit fills me and brings to me a power I never dreamed possible.

The Spirit-filled man or woman is totally given over to pleasing God. The driving force of life is obedience to God – they will sacrifice anything for their Lord. Their thirst for holiness is unquenchable. They are no longer satisfied to be "social drinkers" of the Spirit. Their passion is to be everything God plans for them. They are sold out to God. They are completely "under the influence" of the Spirit of Christ.

Are you contenting yourself with a little sip of God here and there? If not, will you totally sell out to Him and allow His Spirit to fill your heart, mind, soul, and body – all of you, to the extent that you live your daily life totally under His influence?

"Blessed are those who hunger and thirst after righteousness, for they shall be filled."

The images and illustrations of a sacrifice, crucifixion, scrubbing, and filling are biblical ones. Other illustrations, not found in the Scriptures, may also be helpful in understanding sanctification. Let me give two examples:

The Lodestone

Pretend that you hold two pieces of curved metal in your

hand. They look exactly alike. They are of the same weight, material, and size. You cannot tell them apart. After using them for awhile you discover that one of these pieces of metal has a power the other does not. One is a magnet. It has a special quality we call "magnetism." This quality transforms the one piece of metal into a force beyond its inherent properties.

The metal is now naturally attracted to certain other metals. In fact, a tiny needle endued with this force and balanced on a point will invariably indicate the magnetic "north pole." We call this a compass. The force in that tiny piece of metal gives it an "orientation" it had never known before.

So it is with believers who receive God's work of entire sanctification. They now have a force not inherent to themselves. They find themselves habitually drawn toward holiness and obedience. Their desire is pure – 100% magnetized toward Christ. No matter where they are, their inner nature draws them toward righteousness. They have received a new "orientation" in their heart.

"Who Is the Owner Here?"

Imagine, for a moment, that your entire life could be represented as a house. Various rooms would represent the many compartments of your life – your time, talents, appetites, money, future, reputation, thought life, possessions, and dozens of other rooms, closets, and hiding places. Do you have this image in your mind?

Next, Jesus comes along and knocks on your front door. After a period of time, you invite Him to enter and live in the center of your home. As soon as He enters, He goes to work cleaning out some rooms that have been "let go" for years. The house is totally different in only a few weeks. Some neighbors say they don't even recognize it since your Guest came to live with you.

But after awhile you begin to wonder if Jesus is going too far. He keeps moving into new rooms and wants to clean them up too. You were quite attached to some of what He refers to as "this old rubbish." You begin to resist His attempts to change your whole house around. You slip away into one of your favorite rooms where you have kept a number of relics from your old life. Then comes a quiet knock. It is your Guest saying, "I want to clean up that area too." You gather up one or two secret things and stuff them into the closet and, with great enthusiasm, announce to the Lord, "Come in, Lord. You can have everything now."

What does He do? He moves into this room, cleanses it, then walks directly up to the little closet where you have re-treated with a few holdouts. He softly knocks on the closet door saying, "I want all of you – to make you strong." You may struggle for some time in that secret closet. He returns repeatedly, knocking softly.

Then it occurs to you that this man is your friend. He has totally changed your house around, and all the changes were for the better. He loves you more than anyone ever has. He always seems to know what's best. You say to yourself, "What am I doing in here hiding from Him? He knows more about managing houses than I could ever imagine." You fling open the closet door, turn over your few leftovers from your old life to Him. Rushing to your office safe, you remove the title deed to your house and carry it back to Jesus. "Here, take the whole house," you say as you sign over the deed. "From now on it's Yours. You manage it. You direct the remodeling. You decide what must go and what should be added. Right here and now I am signing everything over to You. I'll work for You and let You do whatever You have in mind with this house. It is Yours. I am Yours." This is entire consecration.

Who owns your life?

BIBLE STUDY

1. Read Romans 12:1-2. What aspect of sanctification does this scripture illustrate? In what way?

2. What connection can you see between the verses above and what Paul says in Galatians 2:20?

3. What aspect of sanctification do the following verses illustrate to you?
   a. Colossians 3:5-10

   b. Romans 6:6

   c. Romans 8:14

4. What common theme do these scriptures emphasize?
   a. Acts 2:4   *Holy Ghost - Holy Spirit*

   b. Acts 4:31   *Holy Ghost*

   c. Acts 9:17   *Holy Ghost*

   d. Ephesians 5:18   *Holy Spirit*

5. What aspect of God's sanctifying work do you discover in these verses:
   a. Zechariah 13:1

   b. Ephesians 5:26

For Review and Discussion
1. Which image of sanctification is most helpful to your own understanding? Why?
2. Can you think of some current images and illustrations for sanctification?
3. Why do illustrations help us understand truth?
4. What are the dangers of using illustrations? Can you cite an example of misuse of an illustration?
5. For each image list what part of sanctification it illustrates.

5

Toward Entire Sanctification

The term sanctification refers to the total work of God in making me Christlike. It includes the following:

1. *Initial sanctification* – what God does in me at conversion.

2. *Progressive sanctification* – God's gradual work that helps me grow in grace as a believer.

3. *Entire sanctification* – God's work of cleansing and empowerment when I totally commit myself to Him.

4. *Continual cleansing* – God's daily cleansing of the entirely sanctified believer drawing him or her closer to the image of Christ.

5. *Glorification* – God's final transformation of me at death, preparing me for heaven.

All of these are elements of sanctification. Don't let these terms scare you away! In this chapter we will deal primarily with the first two: (1) God's work of initial sanctification at conversion, and (2) progressive sanctification; gradual growth toward entire sanctification.

This chapter is a little different. It is written in first-person style as the testimony of a woman in her mid-thirties. We will call her Sue.

SUE'S STORY
I. "Satan's Slave"

"Before I was a Christian I was really nothing more than a slave – a slave of Satan. I guess I didn't realize it, but I walked in habitual obedience to Satan's will for my life. I disobeyed God because I chose to. Sin, for me, was not something to avoid. I enjoyed sinning.

"Sure, there were times when I felt twinges of guilt. This was especially true when I hung around Christians very much. I would occasionally wonder if there was something more to life. Yet living it up and satisfying my own human cravings were the true goals of my life. Any thoughts about "turning over a new leaf" would quickly pass as I continued to pursue a life of sin and selfishness.

"Now, I don't mean to say I never did anything good. I did many good deeds. In fact, I was quite respected as a good moral person. I figured I really didn't need Christ. If everybody did their part, the world would be a better place and satisfaction and fulfillment would result. So I busily engaged in a life dedicated to good deeds.

"Then my life began to fall apart. I thought I had everything under control but, little by little, things went haywire. I began to question whether our house, cars, boat, and our summer cottage brought real satisfaction. My marriage hit the skids, and my husband began to threaten to leave. Life began to turn sour.

II. "Conviction"

"I had a neighbor who was always bugging me to go to church. I kept making excuses saying that someday I was going to start attending church. "It's good for the kids," I would say. As meaning drained out of my life, I began to watch these neighbors more closely. They seemed to really 'have it all together.' My idea of Christianity was long faces, stern living, and absolutely no fun. But the family next door was quite cheerful, loving, and had far more fun than our family did.

"One Sunday I woke up early and decided I would start attending church that day. I called my Christian neighbors. (I didn't realize it was 6:30 a.m. and I had gotten them out of bed!) They were enthusiastic and assured me I could sit with them in church.

"I was strangely attracted by the people in that little church. They seemed to have something in their lives that I was missing. When the pastor gave the sermon, it seemed he was talking directly to me. I don't remember what he said. But I began hurting inside like I had never hurt before. I had started to attend church so I could feel better about life, and the opposite happened. I began feeling miserable! Yet, I kept going each Sunday with my neighbors. I gradually realized I needed something they had. Several times the preacher invited people to come up front and pray at the end of the service. I almost went forward. But there was something inside me that held me back. I figured I just wasn't ready yet. I began to read my Bible. It didn't make much sense, but I thought that it might help me out somehow.

"Then one morning I couldn't stand it any longer. When the pastor gave the altar call, I responded immediately. My neighbor went forward with me. That day I confessed I was a sinner and asked God to accept me into His family. I decided to turn away from the sins I was regularly committing. God forgave me and adopted me into His family.

"What a difference! It actually seemed that the entire world was brighter after that day. My husband and children noticed. My boss noticed. And my best friends began asking, 'What happened to you? You're so different.' I told them I had accepted Jesus into my heart. They just shook their heads and figured I had gone off the deep end!

"I still faced problems, but I had a new energy and help in tackling them. I began telling everyone about what God had done for me. And because I had always been isolated by my own bitterness, lots of people noticed the change in me. This excitement and joy continued for more than a year. My husband and several of my old friends began attending church with me – two of them accepted Christ.

"I don't mean to suggest that I was perfect. In fact, I still fell into sin a number of times. But I had a new desire inside to please Christ."

III. "Gradual Growth"

"Then I discovered a new problem. As I read the Bible,

attended Sunday school, and talked to other Christians, I began realizing God's demands were pretty high. I saw He wanted total obedience to His Word. He wanted me to be just like His Son, Jesus. This seemed completely impossible to me, yet I kept sensing this was what He wanted. At conversion I had received a new desire to obey Christ. I was no longer a slave of Satan. But, along with this desire to obey, I still have a spirit of disobedience to God at times. In fact, it seemed there was a constant tug-of-war inside me: the Holy Spirit was on one end, my old desires were on the other, and I was the rope!

"Usually, I sided with my new life in Christ and obeyed Him. But sometimes I sided with my old life and disobeyed the Lord. After these incidents of disobedience, I would feel terrible. I knew that the Bible commanded me to obey, yet often I just wasn't able to pull it off. Some of the 'new convert shine' began to wear off, and I became less intent on sharing Jesus with others.

"Yet, I continued to grow as a Christian. God would make new demands on my life – to give something up, or to begin doing something I ought to be doing, often struggled a long time over these issues. I wanted to please Christ, but I also wanted to keep some practices, thoughts, and habits from my old life. Even when I realized that God wanted me to change, I often resisted Him. These competing desires plagued me, and I sometimes became so weary from the struggle that I was tempted to give up.

"Each time God brought 'new light' to me about something I needed to stop or start I generally responded in three stages.

STAGE ONE – DENIAL. "I remember when He convicted me of a certain habit I had carried over from my old life. My first response was to deny my need. I rationalized my habit as normal, human, and even helpful. I said to myself, 'I'm not perfect – just forgiven.' I had seen other Christians with the same habit. So, I denied having any need.

"However, the Holy Spirit kept knocking. The more I denied the need, the more He gently convicted me. Finally, I realized that continual denial would eventually lead to a cold-hearted experience. I might even lose the relationship I was having with the Lord. So I admitted I needed to change. I said, 'The habit is wrong for me, and I must give it up.'

STAGE TWO – DELAY. "Then I entered the second stage. I had admitted the need for change. Now I tried to delay changing as long as possible. I was convinced, but I had not yet decided to obey. A long struggle followed. I would promise myself to change, but usually I would break the promise. I kept saying, 'Eventually I am going to stop.' But I would emphasize the 'eventually' part!

"The Holy Spirit kept convicting. Now, He had a powerful ally – my mind. I had already admitted need and my mind was made up. The Spirit and my mind worked in concert on my will. The devil encouraged me to continue dragging my feet, not fully obeying what I knew to be God's will. The tension inside me during this second stage was almost unbearable. I knew obedience was the only choice – yet I wanted to continue my habit just a little longer.

"On this particular issue of the wrong habit an interesting event brought about my surrender. Our son takes out the garbage each day when he returns from school. I often have to remind him once or twice of this chore. On one particular day he was especially slow to respond. I had reminded him of his duty four or five times before we sat down to supper. After supper I noticed the garbage was still not carried out and I warned him, 'This is the last time I am going to remind you. Take out the garbage!' He went for his coat, but once again got sidetracked with some of his toys. Later I discovered that the garbage still was not taken out. Needless to say, we had a 'serious talk' (the kind which starts with a spanking!). I explained to my son how continued delaying in obedience eventually becomes disobedience. I was disciplining him, even though he had not outwardly defied my authority. His foot-dragging had, in fact, become disobedience.

STAGE THREE – OBEDIENCE. "Then the Lord made it clear to me. That was exactly what I had been doing with Him! I knew what He wanted, yet I resisted obeying His will concerning this habit. I could no longer deny my need. I was ready to quit delaying. I took the third step – obedience. That very night I surrendered to Him my old habit and asked for deliverance.

"These three stages pretty well describe the next several years of my growth in grace. First, denial of need, then delaying change, and finally obedience. I call it 'walking in the light.' It seems that not long after I would obey God in one area of my life He would move His light forward, showing a new area of need. Then would come a period of conviction and struggle ending – usually – with eventual obedience. After this obedience the full joy of total obedience to Christ would return and would last until the next period of denial or delay.

"But this is not the whole story. It wouldn't be honest to say that I eventually obeyed in all the areas where the Lord convicted. Actually, there were two or three areas where I continued to resist Christ's Lordship. I guess I simply posted a 'no trespassing' sign before these thoughts, habits, or practices and decided to reserve them for myself. This brought a new realization to me: the essential problem in this struggle was my self-will. I wanted to deny need, or delay change. These competing wants in my heart troubled me. I wondered if there was a chance to be delivered from this inclination toward evil. It seemed like I was an ally of the devil. He could count on me to slow, or completely block, my own obedience to Christ.

IV. "A New Vision"

"Then I heard about entire sanctification. I had heard about it before, but this time the truth really came home. I realized that God wanted to be in total command of my life. He wanted to cleanse me of my inclination to disobey and fill me with a power to serve him with all my abilities. I saw, undeniably, that Satan's ally inside me was me! My own self-will repeatedly struggled against the Lord's will for me. I had seen in the Bible God's standard of holiness. I knew I fell far short of what He expected. More than this, I knew that I didn't honestly want to be just like Christ. My desire was divided.

"I began to realize that God was not only convicting me about these few areas of holdout. He was now making claims on something bigger – my will itself. He wanted me to settle this matter of how serious I was about obeying Him – completely obeying His will. At this point it was not a question of surrendering this or that practice, or of being willing to begin a certain habit or practice of righteousness. Now He wanted me to surrender me! He wanted me to totally consecrate myself to Him as the Master of my life. He was asking that I settle this matter, once for all, of who would be 'boss' in my life. A book I read promised that if I really made a 'living sacrifice' – a dedication – of myself to God, He would cleanse me of this rebellious nature.

"At first I doubted that God could deliver me of the inclination to disobey which had so long been part of me. I was, however, quite interested in the notion. I began reading about it, and I talked to several other believers about it. Gradually I began to see this idea in the Scriptures. The Christians I respected most all seemed to have had a time when they 'sold out completely' to Christ. My mind eventually came to believe that God wanted this old consecration and that He would, in fact, do something inside me when He had all of me."

V. "The Consecration"

"I still did not make a total surrender to Christ. I believed I eventually would – yet I delayed. It was then that I realized I was going through the very same stages I so often had followed in committing other areas to the Lord. In each case where I had obeyed I could now see how it was for my own good. God did not want to make me miserable! He wanted to make my life full and joyful. I was working around the house when this fresh realization dawned on me. God wanted all of me because He knows best. I sat down and prayed to God. 'I'm yours – I want you to be the Boss of my life. I no longer will delay consecrating my all to you – from this day forward You have all of me.' Once my will was fully submitted. God cleansed my heart that day of my inclination to disobey Him. And life has been quite different since!"

VI. "In Retrospect"

"Looking back over several years of my gradual growth in grace, I now realize that all the time God had been preparing me for that moment of total surrender to Him. He had progressively drawn me closer to Him in preparation for a new relationship and walk with Him – in full obedience.

Progressive sanctification and entire sanctification are not in competition. They are both elements of God's total plan of making me Christlike. I have several friends who are, right now, in this period of gradual growth. They are winning the battle part of the time. Yet, at other times they are painfully aware of desires inside them which are contrary to God's will. We share together in a regular small-group Bible study, and I can see how God is working. He is bringing them to the place where they are capturing the vision of His Son in such a way that they will someday willingly place their total selves in His hand.

"After all, knowing the kind of person Jesus is, why shouldn't I trust Him with the steering wheel of my life?"

This is one person's testimony. Of course, every individual is different, and your own growth in progressive sanctification may not parallel this account. However, Sue's example illustrates how a believer is transformed at conversion and grows in grace as he or she approaches the decision about entire sanctification.

It is hard to chart how God works. He defies all our systems and diagrams. Like a Father, He leads us along in His light, gently urging us onward. In love He knows what is best for us; and when the truth dawns that He wants our all – enabling Him to be the Master of each life – we can do nothing but place our lives in His hands.

Here's the point of this chapter: If a believer continually obeys the Lord he or she will progressively draw closer to Christ, eventually leading to a decision about total surrender to God. Progressive sanctification leads to entire sanctification.

BIBLE STUDY

Testimonies and individual experience are not an adequate basis for establishing doctrine. Doctrine is constructed as an interpretation of what the Bible says. Yet, personal experience plays an important role in our interpretation of the Word. It is the testing ground of doctrine. Experience is where daily life is lived. Thus, the Bible is literally packed with stories about the lives of real people. God's Word is more than a collection of doctrine. It shares the sometimes intimate details of individual's lives – their successes and failures to follow God's path of holiness. At other points in this book we have studied the teaching (or "didactic") sections of scripture. It is especially appropriate at this point to look at one of the real-life incidents from a Bible character. Turn to Psalm 51.

1. Who wrote this prayer?

2. Can you recall the incident that prompted this prayer? (If not, check out chapters 11 and 12 of 2 Samuel.)

3. What is David asking God to do? (verses 1-2)

4. What does "my sin is always before me" mean? (verse 3).

5. In verse 5 what observation does David make about himself?

6. In verses 7 and 10 David prays for more than forgiveness. What is he asking God to do?

7. What results does he anticipate from both the forgiveness and the cleansing? (verses 8-9,12-13).

For Review and Discussion
1. Describe each of the following aspects of sanctification:
   a. Initial sanctification
   b. Progressive sanctification
   c. Entire sanctification
   d. Continual cleansing
   e. Glorification
2. What was the process Sue went through from being "Satan's slave" through her conversion?
3. As Sue began to grow in grace, God led her to change in several areas. There were the three stages she often went through as she came to obedience. What were they?
4. What relationship is there between progressive sanctification and entire sanctification?
5. Discuss: Is a decision about entire sanctification a natural occurrence for all believers as they grow in grace? Are some people entirely sanctified yet do not know it?

6

What God Does in Sanctification

What does God actually do in me through entire sanctification? What changes occur in my daily life? How will I be different than before? This is the subject of this chapter.

The changes accomplished in me through entire sanctification may be organized into two general categories: (1) PURITY – correction of my inward inclination to disobey God, and (2) POWER – renewed energy for serving God.

All serious students of the Bible and life recognize power and purity as results of an after-conversion commitment to the Lord. But the degree of emphasis on either power or purity varies widely.

One group places heavy emphasis on *purity*, concentrating on the possibility of victory over all willful sin. They emphasize how I may be delivered from the inclination toward sin: lust, covetousness, pride, complacency, envy, impure thoughts, selfish ambition, sinful anger, jealousy, and self-will. This deliverance comes when God does a work in me which corrects and cleanses my inner nature of rebellion. Thus, if my nature is to obey the Lord, I will obey Him to the extent that I comprehend His will.

The second group emphasizes *power* and concentrates on the believer's new involvement in God's work. They are inclined to cite energetic soul-winning as the best evidence of entire sanctification. They emphasize that if I am a Spirit-filled believer, I will be witnessing, active in the church, involved in helping others grow more Christlike, aiding the needy, and actively involved in the world around me.

Our own personal experience may affect what we perceive to be true in this matter. For instance, two individuals who have experienced entire sanctification may strongly disagree on which aspect is predominant.

The first person may have been quite active in the work of the church but has struggled for years with certain secret sins. Finally, after making a total consecration to the Lord, this person's inner nature is cleansed. The most noticeable effect is a deliverance from some sin which had long been a heavy weight. Thus, this person emphasizes purity.

However, a second person's experience is quite different. He or she has never had great trouble with active secret sins, but has been lukewarm, passive, and uninvolved. When this person makes a total dedication to God, he notices a new energy for active involvement in God's work. They naturally assert that power is the dominant expression of this experience. Which is true? Which is the predominant result of entire sanctification – purity or power?

Both are true. They are two sides of the same coin. When God does His work of entire sanctification in me, I find: 1) *a new purity* in my deepest inner being. This results in a definite victory over sin – especially inward sin. But I will likewise experience 2) *a new energy* for doing God's work in the world – winning others to Christ, and helping believers become Christlike. It is not an either/or proposition. Both purity from and power over evil result from this work of God in my heart.

Purity

What kind of purity can I expect? Does God deliver me from all sin forever? Will I be absolutely perfect from that moment? Is this instant Christlikeness? Will there be room for growth? Is this "sinless perfection"?

There is more confusion and misunderstanding over this one point than over any other question relating to holiness.

Some argue that "holiness people" teach an instant perfection; that they say a believer becomes completely perfect – exactly like Jesus Christ – so that there is no need for any further growth – ever. I doubt that this view has ever actually been taught. However, if so, it is resoundingly false.

The root cause of this misunderstanding is confusion over what we mean when we say "it is possible to be delivered from all sin." What do we mean by "sin"?

There are two general ideas of sin. It is vital to understand these in order to see clearly what we mean when we say a believer may be "free from sin."

IDEA 1. This idea of sin focuses on my intentions – or will. I sin when I purposely disobey God – when I decide to disobey. Sin is knowing something is wrong, yet doing it anyway. Or it is knowing something is right, yet refusing to do it. Sin is willfully disobeying God.

IDEA 2. This idea focuses on God's standard of holiness – the law of perfect love. It states that sin is any word, thought, or deed falling short of this standard. Sin includes both voluntary or purposeful transgressions plus the thousands of involuntary times I fall short of God's perfection. Thus, it is easy for those who take this second idea of sin to say they "sin every day in word, thought, or deed." They mean they fall short of Christ's perfect example daily. Of course, in that sense we all do.

When we say God can work in our hearts so that we can live free from all sin, we are speaking about the first idea – willful disobedience (Idea 1). We are talking about a level of living where one's will is so submitted to the Lord's will that, where He clearly leads me, I will follow. Sanctification is the reality of living in total obedience to known guidance from God. It is the confidence that I can cease willful sinning against the Lord, obeying His promptings. I still will fall short of His perfect standard (Idea 2), but I am not held accountable for these involuntary shortcomings, mistakes, or human weaknesses. Though I do not measure up, I am considered blameless, because my will is in submission to the Lord – I am obeying all the light, or leadings, I have. Of course, this blamelessness cannot be used as an excuse for laziness about growth. As God reveals to me areas where I fall short and prompts me to change, I become responsible for this light.

This idea should not be strange to anyone who works with

children. If a 13-month-old child knocks over his milk because of his immature clumsiness, he clearly falls far short of the perfect adult standard of table manners. But no sensible parent would punish a child for this. The parent overlooks this behavior because of the child's stage of development.

However, I have an eight-year-old son. Sometimes he fools around at the dinner table. If, after receiving several warnings, he purposefully reaches out his finger and willfully knocks over his glass of milk, he'd better run!

This is the distinction between the two ideas of sin. The purity of entire sanctification will not prevent me from falling short of God's perfect standard because of my weakness or my stage of growth. However, He is able to purify my heart so that I will not willfully disobey him when I know what He wants.

After following the Lord for awhile, I will recognize that an inclination to disobey the Lord is still present. This inclination leads me into repeated disobedience. The purity of entire sanctification deals with this inclination, or nature – cleansing, purifying, correcting – so that I am able to walk in habitual obedience to the leadings of my Master. Because of my immaturity, inadequacies, and humanness I will still fall short of His perfect standard of righteousness. But, if my will is totally submitted to His, He pronounces me blameless. He is the Perfect Parent.

So, when we emphasize the purity side of entire sanctification, we mean that God is able to cleanse me from the inclination to disobey Him. It then becomes possible for me to live without willful sin. Purity equals obedience.

Power

Our discussion of the power aspect of entire sanctification may be introduced by the following questions:

Q: What is God's work in the world?

A: It is to bring unbelievers to spiritual birth and believers to maturity – to evangelize the lost and to help Christians mature.

Q: What is the greatest hindrance to God's work in the world?

A: Me! Consider it this way. He has no other hands but mine. He has chosen to use believers to accomplish His work of evangelism and discipleship. I am either a help or a hindrance to His glory and work.

First, my sins provide the devil a powerful handle on my back – every time I start moving forward the devil reaches out, grabs the handle, and whispers to my mind, "Where do you think you're going? You know the kind of person you are." Willful sin, whether in action or attitude, gives Satan a powerful handle to restrict our usefulness in God's work. It keeps us from witnessing and helping other believers mature.

Second, I can hinder God's work with selfishness – my self-will. If I am not totally submitted to His will for me, He is greatly hindered in using me. Consider the absurdity of a carpenter attempting to construct a building with a hammer that wanders off every time he sets it down. He spends half his time chasing down the wandering hammer. How that is like us! If we are not totally available and willing to do the Lord's will, He often spends more time "chasing us down" than using us in the world.

Q: Why then does God want us to surrender to His will and receive His empowering work?

A: So He can use us to accomplish His work in the world – evangelizing the lost and lead believers to maturity.

God does not want to cleanse and energize us so He can display us on the shelf for admiration by all – sweet saints, uninvolved with the world. He wants us to be perfectly obedient and to receive power so we can work for Him.

Sanctification is for service. Service means being "sent." Sent where? Sent into a dark, evil world with the pure Light. When Jesus prayed for His disciples' sanctification in John 17, He immediately spoke of their being sent into the world – not to be taken out of it.

The cleansing and power is provided so that I can work in the dirty trenches of daily life, yet remain unspotted; so I may take the light of the gospel and the salt of a Christian witness and be of service in the darkest places. After the power has come, we become more effective witnesses.

Conclusion

Most believers sooner or later recognize one or both of these problems: (1) an inward inclination to disobey the Lord which may result in sinning, especially in sins of attitude and thought; (2) an absence of power and motivation to do God's work in the world – lukewarmness, complacency, and cold-heartedness.

The root cause of these problems is my self-will. The reason I am disobedient is because I decide to disobey. The cause of my complacency is my decision to remain complacent. If God is not the complete Lord of my life, the reason is that I have decided to be my own boss! Here is the essential issue of total consecration – the decision about who will be the boss of my life. I must be willing to make God the Lord of my daily life – to trust Him to perform His work in me. Then I will receive 1) His cleansing from my inward nature to rebel, and 2) a new power and motivation to accomplish His work in this world.

Once this cleansing and energizing is accomplished, I will have an abiding hunger for Christlikeness. This thirst will drive me onward toward the perfect example of Jesus Christ. I will experience ever-increasing joy, fellowship with other believers, love for the lost, a deep settled peace in my heart, and a new energy for evangelism and involvement in the lives of others. God will continue to work in my life, conforming me to the image of His son – in patience, gentleness, humility, satisfaction, meekness, mercy, and love. He constantly will be refining my life as I continue to submit to His will and consecrate my life to His purpose. His cleansing of my inclination to disobedience, and the new power from His Spirit will make a radical difference in my life. This is what God does in entire sanctification – purity from disobedience and power for service.

BIBLE STUDY

1. Turn to Jesus' prayer for His disciples in John 17:6-19 to answer the following questions:

a. Who is Jesus praying for here (verse 9)? Who is He not praying for?

b. What does Jesus ask for His disciples in verse 11?

c. What was the general response of the world to the disciples, according to verse 14? Why?

d. What did Jesus say He was *not* praying for in verse 15?

e. What is His request in verse 17?

f. Following this request what does Jesus immediately talk about in verse 18?

2. Look up each of the following scriptures and write beside each whether it deals with **purity** over sin, **power** for service, or **both:**
   a. Acts 1:8
   b. Psalm 51:7-9
   c. Galatians 5:22-24
   d. Acts 15:8-9
   e. Ephesians 3:16-20
   f. Ephesians 5:25-27
   g. Matthew 3:11-12
   h. Luke 24:49

For Review and Discussion
1. Describe what God does in entire sanctification under the two general categories of "Purity" and "Power."
2. What may cause certain individuals or organizations to give greater emphasis to either power or purity?
3. Which side of God's work in entire sanctification is emphasized most today in your local church? Your denomination? By various para-church organizations? On Christian radio and TV?
4. What are the two differing definitions of sin? When we say it is possible to "live above all sin," of which definition are we speaking?
5. Make a list of what God does NOT do in entire sanctification.

7

How to
Be Entirely
Sanctified

There are two parts to entire sanctification: God's part and man's part. Man's part is consecration and faith. God's part is purifying and energizing.

Down through history believers who wrote, spoke, and testified to this deeper walk with God have variously placed greater emphasis on either God's part or man's part. This is still true today.

Some talk with enthusiasm about God's part. They may give the impression that God does this work in whomever He pleases, whenever He wants to, and perhaps for reasons unknown to us. To them there is little we can do to receive entire sanctification except to become seekers. It may seem that we are supposed to beg God to do something He is reluctant to do. Therefore, we can expect that our seeking will be accompanied by much agony, strain, and pain.

However, others ignore God's part and emphasize man's part — consecration and faith. They take a most logical approach to the whole matter, saying: (a) Carefully consecrate your total life to God. (b) Now, having done that, recognize that the Bible says He will receive your gift and cleanse you. (c) Then, simply believe that the work is completed – you are cleansed. That's it!

Both factors help us see the total picture – God's part and ours. God works in us with our cooperation. We are changed through a partnership with God. He has his part, we have ours.

Only God can cleanse and energize us. We cannot do it ourselves. How many times have we said to wrong attitudes, thoughts, and affections "Be gone!" yet they have remained? How often have we tried to "work up" spiritual energy to witness or to minister to other believers, yet we fail to possess true spiritual power. We cannot cleanse our own sinful "bent." We cannot energize ourselves. This is God's work. Only He can cleanse my heart from its disposition to disobey. Only He can energize my life for evangelism and ministry. It takes His grace, and His power. These are His works.

However, my personal responsibility is to consecrate my life to Him. He cannot do this for me. He will not blast down the door of my life and force faith into my heart. His work is limited only by my own free will – my right to decide. He wants me to dedicate my whole life into His hands. He desires that I trust Him to cleanse and energize me. Yet it will not happen until I decide to consecrate my life to Him and believe His promises. True, in a sense, all I do can be credited to Him – He convicts and tenderly brings me to a place of decision. He is the author of my faith – the earliest conviction is from Him. Yet, it is I, and I alone who must decide.

Sanctification is a partnership – I consecrate and believe; God cleanses and energizes. With my commitment and faith He can purify and empower. In the preceding chapter we examined what God does in entire sanctification – purifying and energizing. Now let us look at man's part – consecration and faith.

Consecration

John's testimony describes consecration:

"After I had walked with God for several years two things gradually became painfully apparent to me: (1) there was power available that I did not have; and (2) I was naturally inclined to disobey the Lord. These realizations came to me gradually, but they grew in strength until I became convinced that I was not where I ought to be – there must be something more.

"I had heard about total consecration and entire sanctification dozens of times. I had always shrugged it off as something I couldn't understand. But last winter it all began to sink in. It was as if a seed of truth had slipped into a crevice of my mind and began to sprout into a tiny bit of faith. I started believing that maybe I could indeed be delivered from my inner rebellion. I began to hope that there was more spiritual power available than I was experiencing. I started reading about the subject and I asked a few friends. Most of them didn't understand sanctification either and couldn't help.

"Then I found Tom. He had always attracted me because of his dedicated work in the church, and I knew how he regularly shared his faith with many people. He was very caring to me. We started meeting each Tuesday for a Bible study. As we studied and shared together, the truth about sanctification unfolded to me in the clearest terms ever. I knew I needed this work and, with Tom's guidance, I finally came to the place where I totally committed my life to Christ – all of me.

"My real struggle surrounded one particular area which I had never allowed the Lord to control. On the Tuesday that God sanctified me I was carefully committing my total life to Him when this one area came to my mind. I quickly passed over it and began listing other things to God. But the Holy Spirit kept bringing my mind back to that one area. I guess it was my real area of holdout.

"Finally, I saw my resistance in this area for what it really was – rebellion against Christ's Lordship. I felt crushed, but I surrendered to Christ in this area and trusted by faith that He had filled me with a new power.

"Though I didn't feel any different right away, within several weeks my life took a totally different direction. As I look back on it now, I wonder why I held out so long. After all, I knew who Jesus was and all He had done for me, so why didn't I trust Him with everything sooner? Why did I think I could do better at managing my life than He could? Anyway, I praise the Lord for sending Tom my way to lead me into this new life of consecration. My life has been wonderfully different ever since."

John's testimony illustrates what God urges us to do. He

77

wants us to make a total surrender of our lives to His leadership and direction. The emphasis is on "total." He wants all of us – our time, talents, thoughts, finances, hopes, aspirations, reputation, hobbies, thoughts, friendships, habits, and future. He wants to be the Lord and Master of every single part of our lives. He knows what is best for us, and He tenderly urges us to turn over to Him our total lives. He wants to direct, guide, use, and change us into the image of His perfect Son. And, with our cooperation, He does this.

Any of us who have walked with God for a time recognize that God regularly urges us to consecrate to Him one or another area. This is the *progressive sanctification* we spoke of earlier. All of us can think of several areas we have committed to the Lord already. What does He do? He invariably moves into that part of our life, rearranging and changing things so that we can now say with assurance, "He knows what is best for me."

Entire consecration is simply the act of giving Christ control of my total life. It is a one-time dedication of my total future life to the Lord. It is covenanting with the Lord always to obey His promptings. It is a commitment – a vow to submit to His will for my life.

Jesus is our example. His prayer in the garden, "Not my will, but yours be done," is the permanent commitment of entire consecration. I am saying, "From this day forward I am taking a vow of total obedience to the Lord." I am promising that whatever He makes clear to me as His will, I will obey. I am deciding to make Jesus the permanent supervisor of all of my life. I am placing everything in His hands – my burdens, my striving, my pains and hurts, and my faults. My total reliance for the remainder of my life will be on Jesus. He will be my consuming passion for living – the absorbing desire of my heart.

This is more than feeling. It is a decision – an act of my will. I am, with firm intentions, placing my "all on the altar" as a sacrifice to God. I want Him – only Him – to rule my thoughts, habits, words, and deeds from now until eternity. I am making an entire surrender, a total abandonment to God – spirit, soul, and body placed under His absolute management. I am making a clear-minded determination to follow Jesus whatever the cost – a vow to a life of obedience. This is total consecration.

Does the idea appeal to you? Are you thinking, "I'd like to do that"? Then why not do it right now? God does not want your total commitment in order to make you miserable. He wants to give you the greatest joy and fulfillment imaginable! Why not trust Him now? Jesus is trustworthy to the extent that you can surrender yourself to Him – so that He will become the Master of every area of your life.

Faith

Faith is man's other part in sanctification. Without faith there is no entire sanctification. We must believe that God will do His work NOW. This is faith.

Faith is not feeling. It is not some sort of bubbly interior excitement which gives us an enthusiastic anticipation that God is going to perform a miracle in our lives.

Neither is faith desire. We may want to be cleansed and energized more than we desire popularity, power, wealth, food, drink – even our next breath. Desire *is* vital, but desire alone is not faith.

Faith isn't hope either. We may someday hope to be entirely sanctified. We could say, "He might do it – "He could do it – it is possible." But this will not bring cleansing to our hearts. This is hope, not faith.

And faith is not fact. We may accept the fact that God cleanses and energizes following our consecration and trust. We may see this truth in God's Word. We may accept it as true, recite it as our creed, and even teach it as dogma; but accepting the fact is not faith.

All of these have a part in our receiving entire sanctification. There is feeling, desire, hope, and acceptance of the factual basis of this work. But none of these are sanctifying faith. We receive God's provisions for us when we reach out in faith and accept them. Sanctifying faith is trusting in Christ's promise now. It is receiving now. It is receiving cleansing and power, not hoping for them. It is more than saying, "I want this work." It is saying, "I receive this work in my heart – right here, and right now."

I may be lavishly loved by another, but until I believe I am loved, that love is never really mine. Belief allows me to receive. Certainly we can understand this in light of the preaching of forgiveness of sins. Some may hear the truth of the gospel for years. But, until they repent and believe that this forgiveness is theirs, they do not receive it. When were you forgiven? Was it when you said, "I think there is something to this"? Was it when you accepted the truth of the gospel as fact? Was it when you began to anticipate that you would one day be forgiven? Was it when you hoped God might forgive you? No. It was when you repented and said, "Forgive me now!" that you received forgiveness. When you reached out on the basis of information you had, believed that God did indeed forgive you, and began acting on that assumption, then you were saved.

So it is with entire sanctification. At the moment I say, "Fill me now," I receive this work. When I reach out on the basis of information I have and believe that God *does* indeed sanctify me *now*, then He accomplishes His work of cleansing and energizing.

When Jesus visited the city of Nazareth, He could do few mighty works. Why? Was it because He was not God anymore? Was it because God is not sovereign? Was it because Jesus was having a bad day? No. It was "because of their lack of faith." They could not believe that this carpenter's son could perform miracles; thus they received no great miracles.

So it is with us. God's work in my life is limited by my own measure of faith. If I doubt that I may be totally cleansed from my inclination to disobey, I will not be cleansed. If I am uncertain about the possibilities of receiving new energy for doing Christ's work, I will not receive this power. God's grace works in my life to the extent of my belief. If I believe He cleanses, He will cleanse. If I believe He energizes, He will energize. My faith enables God's work within me.

Have you made a total consecration of your life to God? Are you His and His alone? If so, then believe He has accepted you now. Believe He has cleansed you now. Believe He has energized you for His work – now! For Christ stands nearby saying, "So be it unto you . . . according to your faith." "*May God himself, the God of peace, sanctify you through and through . . . the one who calls you is faithful and he will do it.*" (*I Thessalonians 5:24*).

BIBLE STUDY

From Romans 12:1-2, think through the following questions:
   a. Who is writing this? (See 1:1)
   b. Is he talking to believers?
   c. What is he urging us to offer to God?
   d. What could it mean to be a "living sacrifice"?
   e. In what ways should we not conform to this world?
   f. How does God "transform" us?
   g. If we make this "living sacrifice" and are no longer conformed to this world because He has transformed our minds, what will we discover?

In each of the following scriptures, what strikes you about the idea of faith?
   a. Luke 17:5-6
   b. 2 Corinthians 5:7
   c. Matthew 8:13
   d. Matthew 9:22,28-30
   e. Mark 9:23,28-29

For Review and Discussion

1. God's part in entire sanctification is cleansing and empowerment. What is man's part?

2. What images from Chapter 4 can you recall which illustrate the idea of consecration?

3. Why is it we cannot receive unless we believe?

4. What relationship do you see between having faith in the possibility of entire sanctification and studying the Bible?

5. If you were to write a little booklet after the fashion of the "Four Spiritual Laws" about entire sanctification, what would you use as your major points?

8

How to Know You Are Sanctified

How can you know that God has indeed entirely cleansed your heart? All you have read so far in this book may seem biblical, logical, and understandable. Yet, your real question is, "How can I know for sure that I am entirely sanctified?"

The answer is that you can know for sure that God has entirely sanctified you. How? There's no "pat" answer, but these questions will help:

1. Have I Made a Total Consecration to Christ?

Can I identify a time when I made a complete consecration of everything to Jesus? Is there a time when I decided to submit to the Lord's will in every area of my life? Do I recall a moment of total surrender similar to either of these below?

THE BIG EVENT. This moment may have been a big event to you. Perhaps you had been struggling against the Lord for many years, resisting His Lordship in one or more areas of your life. Finally, sick of your repeated uncooperative spirit, you yielded everything to Him. It may have been at an altar, maybe your bedside, in the automobile, or under a tree somewhere. But you can recall a time when you made a total surrender to Christ. You asked Him to be the absolute Master of every area of your life. In fact, right now, you may be able to picture the place, perhaps even remember the date, of that final abandonment to God's will – your supreme desire in life. This final surrender may have been accompanied with much joy and relief. To you, it was a monumental big event in your spiritual walk.

THE FINAL STRAW. Then again, this total surrender may not have been so dramatic and monumental for you. You may say the final surrender came after several years of "walking in the light" – simply following after the Master's leadings. Sometimes you resisted the Lord's claims. But eventually you yielded, in obedience to His conviction about some attitude, thought, or practice. Finally, in your growth in grace, you came down to a "final straw" area of commitment. You had been willing to commit everything to the Lord – except this one area of your life. You just couldn't let it go. But He kept urging, and finally you determined that even this would be His. With this area in His hands He then had all of you – you had totally submitted your will to His.

Regardless of which story comes closer to your own experience, can you say that there was a time when you totally submitted your will to Christ and determined to obey Him in every way from that day forward? Was there a time when you settled, once and for all, the question of who would be the boss in your life?

The first question is focused on consecration. Can you recall a time when you made a total consecration of every area of your life to God's absolute will? Do you know right now that your will continues to be in total submission to His? Is He the boss of all of your life?

2. Do I Have Power over Willful Sin?

Can I say there is no willful disobedience in my life right now? Is there something God has clearly convicted me is wrong, yet I continue to do it? or say it? or think it? Is there anything I know with certainty that God is directing me to do, yet I am refusing to do it? Am I deciding to disobey the Lord in any area of my life?

If there is willful sin in your life, it blocks off the channel of assurance. If you know that you are purposefully disobeying the Lord in any way, your assurance will be replaced by doubt. Assurance and disobedience do not dwell together well.

In fact, if there is willful sin in your life, you should concentrate on dealing with your rebellion to the Lord, rather than on seeking some assurance that you have been cleansed. If you settle the central issue of "Who will be boss?" and yield completely to Christ's Lordship, then the cleansing, power, and assurance will come. Assurance is a by-product of total surrender, not an end in itself. So, if you are reading this and recognize there are areas in your life where you are rebelling against God's will, you need to focus on submission, not on assurance.

This question, "Do I have power over willful sin?" deals with obedience. Can you say with certainty that you are obeying God in everything He has spoken to you about?

3. Have I Experienced a Distinct Increase in Love?

Has God changed my "orientation" toward others so that my heart and will are completely committed to love them? Am I becoming "perfect in love" as Christ is?

Being perfect in love is more than cleansing from bitterness, grudges, malice, ill will, envy, hate, and other inward sins, though this happens. Beyond this freedom, His cleansing and energizing brings a distinct increase in actual love for other people — not just likable people, but those who are unlikable — even those who call themselves our enemies.

This love is more than a feeling. It is a mind-set, a commitment of the will to love. It is saying, "I shall love others, for that is what the Lord wants me to do." It is active, pursuing the best for others in each case. It is compassionate — selflessly aiding others without concern for personal return.

Now, you may not immediately notice what is happening to you. Then you begin to realize that a particular bitterness you had carried against someone is gone. Next you may find yourself saying and doing things quite out of character for you — acts and words of love for others which were not your usual behavior in the past. You may not fully recognize this increase in love for several weeks or months. But, if you have surrendered your self-will to Christ, He will do a work in your heart that will result in a new love for others which is not naturally inherent.

After complete consecration to Christ, you will experience a distinct increase in your love for others. Bitterness, envy, malice, ill will, and grudges toward others will disappear. A new inner commitment to love others will sprout and continue to grow in your heart. Can you recall a time when you settled the question of who would be boss in your life, and then received a new spiritual energy? Might we name this energy . . . "love"?

4. Is Obedience the Consuming Passion of My Heart?

The following testimony helps explain what we mean by the "consuming passion of my heart." This letter is an answer to the question: "You say you're sanctified. Are you perfect?"

"What a tough question, 'Am I perfect?' How can I answer it? If I say, 'Yes,' I set myself up as a target. Anything that looks questionable to anyone can be seen as evidence that I am indeed not perfect. And, if I say 'no', then it may be said that no work has then been done in me. So I shall answer you by saying 'yes and no.' Be patient, I am not avoiding the question. I will tell you what I mean.

"I am not as perfect as Jesus Christ, the Heavenly Father, the angels, Adam and Eve (before the Fall), or even as I will be after death. I fall short of God's perfect standard of performance every day. And I still have a long road to become everything that God yet intends for me. In these ways I am not perfect. Then in what way could I say I am perfect?

"First, let me say that John Wesley didn't like the word, and I don't either. There are better words to describe this life. The word has an egotistical flavor to it. It sounds like something the Pharisees might say – quite the opposite of what sanctification is all about! Perfect gives most of us the impression that there is no need for growth or maturity – that everything is finished and complete. So, I don't use the term myself. But, since you asked specifically, I will answer specifically. In what sense is an entirely sanctified person perfect?

"One windy March day I settled the issue of Christ's control of my life and placed my total life in His hands. I decided that the Lord would sit at the steering wheel of my life. That decision meant I would no longer run the affairs of my life for my own benefit.

"I noticed several changes following this 'final wrestling match' with the Lord. But the greatest permanent change occurred in my heart. Ever since that day I have had a consuming passion to obey Christ. He has become the central force of my life, I have this new thirst for holiness. In a sense I am now a slave to Jesus Christ, like the 'love slave' in the Old Testament. I decided at one point to submit to His will in everything for all eternity. The issue is settled.

"I don't mean to suggest that I always feel on top of things and full of boundless energy. In fact, the feeling is not nearly as important as the matter of my will. I have decided He is Lord of my life. No matter how I feel, I will obey Him. I don't want to suggest that I achieve the standard my heart desires. I often fall short of what He wants me to be. But I continue to have this passion to be like Jesus. Holiness is not just high priority for me, it is the central priority of my life, around which all other priorities orient.

"This is the only perfection I testify to. It is a *perfection of intention.* It is a dominant hunger for holiness and obedience. Something happened to me, two years ago this March, which totally reoriented my priorities. Obedience to Christ is now the central purpose of my life."

This letter of testimony illustrates the fourth question: Do I have an undivided heart? Can I say that my heart is magnetized toward Christ? Am I fully committed to obedience? Is Christ's will the central focus of my life? What do I want most out of life? Is it obedience to His will?

5. Does the Spirit Witness to My Heart?

This final question is most interesting. It relates to the "witness of the Spirit" aspect of my sanctification. We may be familiar with this idea as it relates to conversion: How do I know that I am a Christian? There is the evidence – the promise of forgiveness, the fact of my repentance, my changed life. Yet there is more. Down deep inside me the Holy Spirit confirmed to my heart that He has adopted me into God's family. This is not a feeling; it is an inner certainty and conviction, not totally dissimilar to how I know I am in love. I just know it – for sure.

The witness of the Spirit to my entire sanctification is like this. I may have the evidence of my total consecration, the power I have over willful sin, a new love for others, and a consuming passion to please Christ, but there is more. Somewhere along the line the Holy Spirit will witness to my heart that He has indeed cleansed and energized me, and I am continuing in the sanctified life.

This witness may not come immediately. It could be days, weeks, or months before the Spirit convinces me of what God has already done. But the witness will come. The coming of this witness is entangled with my faith. As long as I doubt that the work is complete, my faith is short of sanctifying faith.

And the witness may not remain at the same intensity. It may sometimes be stronger, and at other times weaker. But the Holy Spirit is faithful and He will convince, even reconvince, of His work in my heart.

I can be sure – a deep settled surety that God has cleansed and energized me. His Spirit will testify to my heart that He has done this work.

Conclusion

I can know that the Lord has entirely sanctified me. First, I should examine the evidence:

1. Have I made a total consecration to Christ?
2. Do I have power over willful sin?
3. Have I experienced a distinct increase in love for others?
4. Is obedience the central focus of my life?
5. Does the Spirit witness to my heart?

If my answer to these questions is in the affirmative, I can say with assurance that the Lord has entirely sanctified me. All praise to Him!

However, if in being totally honest, I had to say, "This is not true of me," then I should not be worrying about assurance of sanctification but should focus on the problem pointed up by the questions I answered "no" to:

1. Are there areas in my life not fully consecrated to the Lord? Why do I hold them back?
2. Am I guilty of willfully disobeying the Lord against clear light He has given me? I should confess my sin, repent, and turn away from that disobedient thought, word, or act.
3. Do I possess bitterness, envy, ill will, malice, or an unforgiving spirit toward anyone else? Is my love wanting? I should likewise confess these sins and turn away from them. If I have these attitudes, it is because I have chosen to have them; my will is the problem.

4. Is my heart divided – partly pulling toward pleasing Christ yet partly pulling toward self and sin? I should settle once and for all this matter of authority in my life. Why wait?

5. Can I answer the first four questions affirmatively, yet still have not received the witness in my heart that God has done this work? If so, then I should patiently wait for His own good timing, all the while making sure I keep myself on the altar of total surrender.

BIBLE STUDY

This book has invited you, the reader, to turn to your own Bible and study the matter of sanctification in light of God's Word. The idea of entire cleansing and energizing is found in the Scripture. As you study on your own, you will repeatedly discover the various strands which make up this truth, convincing evidence that the doctrine of holiness is based on God's Word and not on man's "proof-texting" out of the Bible.

Today's Bible study is in Romans, chapter 6. You may wish to use the following questions as you study this chapter:

Romans 6:1-18

1. What should a believer's attitude be toward continued sinning? (Verses 1-2)

2. Why should believers not be sinning? (Verses 2-4)

3. What does the writer mean by the "old self"? (Verse 6)

4. What does Christ's crucifixion have to do with our "old self"? (Verse 6)

5. What do you think the phrase "the body of sin might be rendered powerless" means? (Verse 6)

6. In what way are we "dead to sin"? (Verses 7-10)

7. The term "count" or "reckon" is an accounting term. What does it have to do with what we must do concerning sin (verse 11)? (You may want to look up these words in the dictionary.)

8. Can you see a call for entire consecration in verses 12-14?

9. What two options for slavery are mentioned in verses 15-16?

10. What have these believers become "set free from"? (verses 17-18).

11. What kind of new slavery have they experienced? (verse 18).

12. What similarities do you see with this consecration and that of the love-slave found in Deuteronomy 15:12-17?

For Review and Discussion
1. This chapter cites five evidences of entire sanctification. Can you list them?
2. What key word would you select for each of these?
3. What other evidences of entire sanctification are there?
4. What advice would you give to a person who thinks he is entirely sanctified, but he is not sure?
5. Compare the evidence of conversion with that of entire sanctification. What are the similarities? Differences?

9

Dialogue on the Sanctified Life

Confusion about the sanctified life abounds. Some folk have painted an absurd picture of what it means to be sanctified. Many have the idea that this walk with God makes a person some sort of spiritual superman, raising him above all human frailties and temptations and providing a life of constant exultation and joy. This is not true.

This chapter is written in dialogue style between two individuals about the sanctified life. The first (JL) has been a believer for eight years and recently made a total consecration to God and was entirely sanctified. Yet, there are still many questions. The second, (SB), is JL's spiritual mentor, and has been walking in the sanctified life for several years. This is their conversation:

Testifying

JL: "It has been several months now since I experienced God's sanctifying work in my life. I have shared this with several of my close friends, but I am not sure how widely I should broadcast it. I almost wonder if it is something like humility – once you claim it you no longer have it. What do you think? Should I testify to entire sanctification?"

SB: "Sure, but with great care. Probably you should not talk about it to an unbeliever at all. They do not have the spiritual perception to understand sanctification. And, in speaking to believers, be careful to avoid the appearance of spiritual boasting. When you testify, speak with humility, seeing that all the glory goes to God. Nevertheless, do speak up, for two good reasons: (1) It will affirm the experience to you — just as public confession about conversion was a great aid to your life. (2) It will be a great encouragement to other believers who are seeking a deeper walk with God. Certainly you should tell others. Just use discretion and care."

Temptation

JL: "I'm beginning to get confused on one particular point concerning sanctification. I think I really need help. Last month I was sure God had cleansed me. I am beginning to wonder about that now."

SB: "What makes you question that this work was done in your heart?"

JL: "Well, for a month or so it seemed things were going well — I didn't even give the slightest consideration to some of the wrong thoughts and attitudes I had. It seemed like I would not even be tempted again. Then, during this last month I have been tempted severely to think the same kind of thoughts as before. And I've been tempted to develop some of those sinful inner attitudes again. How could I be sanctified when I am tempted like this again?"

SB: "Have you given in to these temptations?"

JL: "No, I haven't. But even when I resist them, they often do not go away. It's like a giant battle, and I am getting shot at from all sides."

SB: "Why have you resisted so far?"

JL: "I want to be obedient — I remember what I was like last year at this time, and I want no part of my former defeated life. In fact, that's what is distressing me. I fear I might give in and wind up even less happy than before."

SB: "Don't worry so much. Take heart that you have not given in to these temptations. You have committed yourself wholly to Christ and the matter is settled — you have decided to obey Him. But no experience on earth can place you beyond temptation. There may be periods of peace which remain for days, weeks, or even months. You might be lulled into thinking you will no longer be tempted. How wrong! You will repeatedly be tempted. In fact, it is quite possible that Satan will double his attacks on a totally committed person. So, don't be defeated by temptation. A servant is not above his master – Jesus was tempted; you will be too.

JL: "Then what was I cleansed from? If I am tempted by something, I must want to do it or it wouldn't be tempting. So how could I have been cleansed from my nature of disobedience?"

SB: "You must not confuse temptation with the evil nature. Take Jesus for example. His nature was pure. He was in the garden and the devil was tempting Him to avoid the cross. Did he want to be crucified? Was He saying to himself, 'This is what I really want to do?' No. His humanness drew back from the painful experience before Him. His natural human inclination was to avoid pain. There was still a struggle. In fact, He struggled so much He sweated drops of blood. Yet the matter was settled from the start. His will was so completely committed He could pray 'Not my will, but yours be done.' His natural body resisted, but His heart was set toward total obedience to God.

"When I am tempted, I try to remember Jesus' example. He was without an evil inclination, yet He wrestled to the point of sweating blood. Entire sanctification does not deliver you from human desires – fear of pain, desire for acceptance, sexual drive, and so forth. It cleanses your nature so that you are able to keep from abusing or perverting these natural desires, becoming disobedient. When your will is set (you have settled the matter of total obedience to God) and even when great seasons of temptation come, you can know that the whole business is settled. Then when the curtain comes down, you will have resisted because the central principle of your life is 'not my will, but God's be done.' "

Keeping Entirely Sanctified

JL: "Like I said, the life of total obedience to the Lord is so rich for me that sometimes I'm afraid I may lose this walk with Christ. Have you ever felt that way?"

SB: "Sure. In fact, one time I did lose this walk with Christ."

JL: "How did it happen? How did you get back on track?"

SB: "Well, it's a long and painful story. I settled this whole thing of Christ's Lordship a long time ago. I had placed all of my life in Christ's hands. Eleven months later I began to drift into casualness. The zeal I had began to diminish. I quietly began to take one or two things back off the altar of total consecration. They were areas I had trouble with before. The Spirit convicted me, but I did not listen. Soon I was in purposeful disobedience to the Lord. My love began to dry up, and I became unconcerned and critical again.

"Then I went to a renewal retreat in the mountains of Colorado, and the Lord made it clear to me what I was doing. I was resisting His will in my life. He and I both knew it. The blessing was gone. That night beside my bed in Colorado, I sobbed out my confession to Jesus. I had taken myself back from His leading and control. I was resisting and rebelling against the Lord – sinning. That night I placed myself on the altar of consecration again, and the blessing of this obedient life returned.

"I learned an important lesson through that painful time. Consecration is more than a once-for-all event. Retaining entire sanctification is done the same way we receive it. I keep sanctified by keeping my 'all on the altar.' I keep sanctified by keeping faith. It is a continuous act of consecration and a continuous life of faith. So, I would advise you to worry less about losing what you have and concentrate more on keeping your all on His altar and keeping your faith in His work vibrant."

Growth

JL: "You are suggesting that the life of entire sanctification is ongoing – it is not static or fixed at some level of perfection that will never change. Right?"

SB: "By all means. In fact, many are confused in thinking that once a person is entirely sanctified, that's it for them for life – they are in no need of any more growth. This is untrue.

JL: "I sure know how far I have to grow. In fact, I sense the disparity between my life and the perfect standard of Jesus Christ more than ever."

SB: "Exactly. Entire sanctification cleanses me from my inclination to disobey, and empowers me for service. It does not make me into an angel. He brings instant purity, but maturity comes slowly.

"The sanctified life is expandable, like the annual rings

on a tree. A 14-year-old tree can be said to be a 'perfect' tree. Yet, 30 years later it will have grown to be much larger, stronger, and more mature. It will now have 44 annual rings. We may be pronounced 'perfect' at an early stage of our Christian maturity, but there are many 'annual rings' of holiness the Lord wants to add to our lives as we grow. The Bible repeatedly instructs us to "put on" compassion, kindness, humility, gentleness, patience, love, peace, self-control, and other qualities of Christlikeness. At entire sanctification all of these fruits of the Spirit-filled life are present, but they are expandable. Our love, kindness, and deeds of mercy, may increase every day we are on this earth, and perhaps through all eternity. The life of holiness is expandable. In fact, we should grow even more after this work is done, because now we are in total submission to His will for us. His will for us is always growth."

JL: "The biggest difference in my life now is this fresh hunger I have for Christlikeness. That is why these temptations have been so troublesome – I want so badly to be like Jesus that any temptation to disobey is shattering to me. When I examine my life over the past few months, I realize what a great leap my walk with Christ has taken. Sure, I realize I still have a long way to go. Yet, I have experienced such dramatic growth during these months! It is exciting to imagine what the Lord will accomplish in me over the rest of my lifetime."

SB: "If we keep walking in total obedience to Him, our lives will become more mature as a result of His love at work in our lives. He is the Master Potter. Obedience is the key to the sanctified life."

Self-Control

JL: "I want to change the subject a bit. Let's talk about self-control. I was reading in Galatians 5:22 the other day, and one fruit of the Spirit is 'self-control.' I have been talking about being 'Spirit-controlled,' but how is this different from self-control? A friend of mine says the idea of being Spirit-controlled sounds like people becoming spiritual robots. What is the connection here between self-control and Spirit-control?"

SB: "It is a cycle – they feed each other. The Spirit will not control anything in my life without my permission. As I exercise self-control, submitting myself to the Spirit's control,

He works in me to accomplish His will. As the Spirit moves throughout my life, a part of the 'fruit' of His work is self-control. So the cycle goes on – the more I control myself submitting to Christ, the more He controls me, resulting in the fruit of more self-control. Like so much in the Christian life, this is a partnership with God. As we continually submit to Him, it is easier to continue to submit to Him in greater and greater degrees. The result is a continual growth toward Jesus.

The opposite is true as well. Disobedience and lack of self-control result in the fruit of rebellion, which produces the by-product of greater disobedience and rebellion which then goes on to catapult a person into a downward spiral of sinfulness, winding up in his becoming completely reprobate."

JL: "Then it is not a matter of choosing between self-control and Spirit control is it? Both factors work together to help me grow more like Christ."

SB: "Yes, and the central issue preceding all this is who is the boss of my life. If God is the Master of my life, I will find new self-control through His cleansing power, and this will enable me to continually submit to His will."

Cautions

JL: "I have a growing realization that there are some inherent dangers in this closer walk with Christ. You have already cautioned me about the attitude I might portray in testifying to this experience. What other cautions would you suggest?"

SB: "First, I would say watch for pride. You may have experienced such a dramatic change in your life that the devil's best snare is to encourage you to begin thinking of yourself as better than other believers – as one of God's favorite children. Avoid spiritual pride at all cost. Continually give all the glory to God in humility. Be careful of talking down to those who do not understand or who disagree with you on some point. I think one of the best definitions of humility is 'teachableness.' Continually develop a spirit of teachableness. Don't assume you're always right and that everyone must now line up and become like you. Listen. Learn. Ask questions. Keep a spirit of humble meekness about your spiritual walk."

JL: "What else?"

SB: "Be careful of going off the deep end emotionally. A person who is in total submission to God has a new spiritual sensitivity. However, you can run off on a tangent supposing dreams, visions, impressions, prophecies, languages, and ideas are from God. In fact, your own imagination may be the source. All through history some who have experienced this second work in their life have tended to fly off into some sort of bizarre emotionalism. Be careful of this. Much damage has been done to the teaching of the doctrine of holiness by these extremists. The antidote – stick to the plain truths of scripture as the central focus of your life."

JL: "I recognize this sideline. I have an aunt who was just an average Christian. She got into a small-group Bible study and received some sort of new "special baptism" as she called it. She went right up the wall emotionally and finally wound up in all kinds of spiritism. She even tried to make contact with the spirits of the dead. So, I know I should avoid pride and extreme emotionalism. Is that it?"

SB: "No, there are dozens of other bits of advice to those who are walking in total submission to Christ. We don't have time to cover them all. However, one of the most important is to continually strive for the disciplined life. Some tend to think that their state of grace is so high they are beyond the need of self-disciplined habits. Since they 'pray always,' they need no particular time for prayer. Or, since 'to the pure all things are pure,' they can participate in questionable activities or read material of dubious moral quality with no ill effects. Remember, the devil does not scratch you off his list when you are wholly sanctified. In fact, he may place you at the top of his hit list!

"There are a few others. For instance, be especially on guard for sins of omission – things God prompts you to do which you are not doing. We can be disobedient to God as easily through not doing right as through doing wrong. Prayerlessness is certainly such a sin.

"And be constantly on the watch against letting Jesus be pushed out of the center of your life. Don't let anything begin to slip in and take dominance in your life again. Concentrate on continual consecration to the Lord. Obedience to Him must be your central goal in life.

"Keep your relationships with others in loving harmony. Never – absolutely never – break a relationship with another believer. Nothing will rob you of a sanctified life more quickly than a broken relationship with a brother or sister.

"Finally, live an exemplary life in all aspects. Watch your

example in spending money, in conversation with others, in sharing your faith, in the manner of your dress and actions, in your faithfulness in attending church services, and in serving the needy. Make sure everything you do and say will be an example of holiness and will bring honor to the cause of Christ. If you continually draw close to Him, He will draw near to you and you will have even greater power as you become more like Him."

BIBLE STUDY

1. According to 1 Corinthians 15:10, what kind of attitude should we have in testifying to a work God has done in our lives?

2. Find four truths about temptation from 1 Corinthians 10:12-13.

3. What kind of picture of the expanding Christian walk do you see in 1 Corinthians 9:24-27? What are some ways to control our bodies?

4. What limitation does the treasure of this experience have according to 2 Corinthians 4:7? What is the advantage of this to God?

5. Write 2 Corinthians 3:18 in your own words.

6. From Hebrews 12:1-4 list five rules for effectively running the "spiritual race."

For Review and Discussion
1. What cautions should be observed in testifying to entire sanctification?
2. If an entirely sanctified person is still tempted, what real difference does sanctification make in his life?
3. Can a person lose entire sanctification? How? How is this life then recovered?
4. In what way can an entirely sanctified person still grow?
5. What advice would you give an entirely sanctified person? What should he or she be on guard against?

10

Holiness and Temperament

What is temperament? Does entire sanctification give us a new temperament? Will it make a boisterous extrovert into a calm and quiet individual? Or are we "stuck" with our individual temperaments with little hope of changing in this life? What does holiness have to do with temperament? These are questions we will examine in this chapter.

What Is Temperament?

The idea of people possessing differing temperaments is more than a thousand years old. In this generation Tim LaHaye has popularized the ancient theory that all people fall into one of four basic temperament types. Temperament is not character. Character refers to traits developed through personal discipline, training, and God's grace. Honesty, loyalty, kindness, and patience are character traits. No person may say he or she is born with a natural tendency to these traits of character.

Temperament, on the other hand, is a natural inclination. We are born with it. Our temperaments are set in our genes and honed by our environment and childhood. Temperament is what makes some of us outgoing or extroverted, and others quiet, shy, and introverted. Temperament is what makes one child bold and aggressive while his sister or brother is shy and dependent.

One analysis of temperament types deals with four basic temperament categories. These categories may be named variously, yet they are generally quite similar. In this chapter we will use four individuals to illustrate these basic types of temperaments. Please meet JoAnne, John, Sharon, and Jim:

JoAnne. When JoAnne enters a room of people, she seems to "fill it up" with her personality. She is talkative, personable, and outgoing. She loves people and seldom meets anyone whom she considers a stranger. She flits from one small group to another, chattering with each person as if that person is her very best friend. She easily gathers people around her and rallies them to a task – she is frequently called on to be a leader of something new. Where there's action, you'll find JoAnne at the center of it.

John. Few people are as forceful as John. He seems to wind up as the leader of every group he gets involved with. John is a hard driver, likes to get things done, a builder. He has no trouble making decisions – even for other people. Most folk recognize that his natural abilities equip him to be the boss of just about anything. He likes to try new things and is always launching some new project at home, at work, or in his local church. John is respected – even feared – by most people.

Sharon. Sharon works with fifth graders all week, then spends most of the weekend working with children in her local church. She is calm, easygoing, and well-liked by just about everyone. She is systematic and so well organized that others marvel at the quantity of work she gets done with so little fuss. Though she does not get involved with everything, she will carry through on any commitment she makes. Her loyalty is deep.

Jim. Jim is the opposite of JoAnne. He doesn't prefer to be in large groups; and when he is forced into one, he would rather sit to the side and keep quiet. He is extremely creative, artistic, and is a deeper thinker than any of his associates. He is always thinking of a better way to do things. He blossoms into a chattering speech when someone talks about philosophy and theory. Jim is extremely sensitive. People sometimes hurt him without even knowing it. When he is "up," he can produce

100

more ideas in a few minutes about how to do something than most people can in several hours. He is definitely the most creative person in his group. These four – JoAnne, John, Sharon, and Jim – represent the four basic temperament types. Jim is a writer and part-time artist; Sharon is a schoolteacher; John is a boss; and JoAnne is a district sales manager for a home sales company. Using the oldest categories of temperament types, JoAnne would be a "sanguine," John a "choleric," Sharon a "phlegmatic," and Jim a "melancholic."

Each of us usually leans toward one of these basic types of temperament. Of course, none of us are 100% of any one temperament. Generally, we have a dominant temperament type, a secondary type, while the other two remain recessive. Such temperament traits are a result of our inherited characteristics and environmental shaping. Each of us is different and has his own particular strengths and weaknesses.

The Other Side of Temperaments

So far we have only spoken about strengths of these four temperament types. On the other side there are corresponding weaknesses or "besetting sins" for each temperament type. JoAnne, John, Sharon, and Jim are all members of a "Covenant cell group." One week they were studying the idea of besetting sins, and each requested prayer support for the areas where they are tempted most. What were these requests?

JoAnne, the outgoing sales manager, confessed she was undisciplined in her devotions, not submissive to authority, and feared that she was often too egocentric.

John, the boss, confessed a serious problem at home with anger, a tendency to be proud, and that he often was dominating, pushy, and insensitive with his employees at work.

Sharon, the teacher, asked for prayer relative to her inclination to be stingy, her fearfulness of launching out to do new things for the Lord, and her extreme defensiveness whenever anyone offered her suggestions or advice – especially her husband.

Jim, the writer-artist, expressed concern for his tendency to be critical of others – always thinking of how they "ought to" do things, for his moody behavior at home, and his negative attitudes of doubt.

Holiness and Temperament

Now, what does all this have to do with holiness and entire sanctification? Does sanctification change our temperaments? Will JoAnne become quiet and submissive when she is sanctified? Will God make John easygoing like Sharon? Will sanctification make Sharon aggressive and generous? Will the Holy Spirit even out Jim's moods? What relationship does entire sanctification have to temperaments?

1. **Entire sanctification does not destroy our natural temperaments.** Extroverts do not become introverts. Pessimists do not become optimists. Aggressive, high-powered people do not become passive and shy. Sanctification results in a refinement and a purification of our natural temperaments. In sanctification, God harnesses and redirects our strengths. He provides new power over our besetting sins. God needs an infinite variety of personality qualities to do His work. He is not in the business of making cookie-cutter believers.

2. **God's cleansing will bring a new power over besetting sin.** This is one of the reasons people differ so widely as to what God actually does through entire sanctification. JoAnne may claim God gave her new self-discipline and a spirit of submission. John realizes a fresh love and sensitivity for his employees. Sharon experiences a new motivation to get involved. And Jim has a newfound power over his critical spirit. Each has experienced the same work of God. Yet, the area of cleansing is different and quite related to his or her temperament traits. Whatever our besetting sin, God wants to cleanse our hearts of the inclination to it. He does this through entire sanctification.

3. **As we grow in the sanctified life, God continues to mold our personality strengths.** He will help JoAnne harness her extrovertism to make her a better witness for the gospel. He will gradually channel John's energy into leading other believers to accomplish His work. He progressively strengthens Sharon's loyalty so that she becomes the "right-hand woman" of the church. He will keep developing Jim's creativity so that it is directed into practical and helpful work, and not mere theory. All this is accomplished as a sanctified person daily submits to the Lordship of Christ. Heart purity may be the work of an instant. But continual growth in Christian personality is a lifetime work.

4. **Not only does the Lord develop the strengths of our**

own temperament, He also brings us strengths not inherent to our own basic personality. This too is an ever-expanding work of the Holy Spirit. As we submit daily to His work and leadings, He begins to bring strengths to us which are largely foreign to our natural temperament. For instance, as JoAnne is totally obedient to the Lord, she may become a leading example of self-discipline and submission – even though her basic temperament does not incline her to be so. A bossy John may become exceptionally sensitive and loving toward other people. A defensive Sharon may become extremely open and vulnerable. And an unsociable Jim may become quite friendly to a neighbor he wants to win to Christ.

So while the initial work of sanctification immediately impacts us regarding our besetting sins, God works progressively at developing our strengths throughout our entire lives. This expanding work will bring personality strengths to us which are not even inherent in our natural temperament.

5. **Perfect Christlikeness is found in the "Body of Christ."** Evangelist Jimmy Johnson is adept at making this truth clear. His idea: (A) Christ was the perfect personality – He exhibited all the strengths of all four temperament types. (B) None of us will ever arrive at this absolute perfection of personality on earth. (C) Unbelievers must somehow, somewhere see this perfect Christlikeness. (D) Perfect Christlikeness is found in the church – the Body of Christ.

As we gather together as a Body, each with our own unique strengths, Christ is seen. And, just as examining a finger or an ear does not give us a total picture of a human body, so examining one individual believer will not give a total picture of what Jesus is like. Yet, the corporate Body of believers illustrates pure Christlikeness – one believer illustrates one strength and another believer exemplifies a different strength.

This "corporate holiness" does not get us off the hook relative to personal holiness. On the contrary, our motivation to become Christlike is greater as we recognize that we are part of a grand Body of believers who together do, in fact, illustrate all the strengths of Jesus Christ. In this sense we are truly part of the "Body" of Christ.

Thus, any search for a perfect example of holiness will lead the seeker to both the Word of God and to the Body of Christ. In the Word of God we see Jesus the perfect example. When the Body of Christ is taken as a total group, we catch a glimpse of the same traits of Jesus Christ.

BIBLE STUDY

1. Read Acts 8:1-2 and Acts 9:1-2. What kind of person was Saul/Paul?

2. Now read Galatians 2:11-14 answering the following questions:
   a. Who is speaking here?
   b. How did Paul "oppose" Peter?
   c. Why did he oppose him so strongly?
   d. What effect did Peter's action have on others?
   e. What does Paul's action have to do with his temperament?

3. Read Acts 15:36-41. Answer the following:
   a. What did Paul want to do here?
   b. What brought on this sharp disagreement?
   c. What resulted from their disagreement?
   d. What insight from Paul's temperament do you have from this Scripture?
   e. In Acts 20:36-38, what evidence of sanctification do you see of Paul's rugged choleric temperament?

For Review and Discussion
1. What are the four basic temperament types? With which one or two do you identify?
2. What are the natural strengths of each of these types?
3. What are the inherent weaknesses of each?
4. If entire sanctification does not totally change our natural temperaments, how does it relate to temperaments?
5. What connection do you see between temperaments, the Body of Christ, and holiness?

11

Sanctification and Stewardship

Why would a book on holiness devote a chapter to the subject of stewardship? What connection is there between holiness, or entire sanctification, and stewardship?

The idea of stewardship originates with the ancient practice of placing the management of wealth in the hands of another. Abraham, for instance, possessed great holdings – flocks, herds, servants, and eventually land. The common practice was to place all these holdings in the hands of a competent manager who would oversee the day-to-day operation of the business. In Abraham's case, Eliezer was named as the manager, or steward of his operation. Great trust and authority were vested in these stewards, especially when the owner was on a far journey and the total control was in the hands of the steward for months or even years.

In ancient literature, there seems to be no "Steward's Code," though other professions had such codes. Yet, if we think of an owner preparing to take a long journey, and if an agreement were to be written between these two men, we can easily imagine the following:

STEWARD'S AGREEMENT
1. The owner hereby places all his belongings, namely his

houses, flocks, servants, fields, and all other tangible property into the hands of the steward for his management.

2. The steward shall manage, oversee, and superintend the day-to-day operation of said possessions.

3. All daily decisions regarding the receiving of income, expenditure of funds, and investment of assets shall be in the hands of said steward who shall at all times make such decisions for the best interest of the owner.

4. Guidance for establishing the best interests of the owner shall be determined by: (1) the past close personal knowledge of the owner by the steward, and (2) regular examination of the *Book of Values* written by the owner and left with said steward.

5. The steward is expected to produce an increase in the net worth of the possessions during the time of his managerial responsibility. The owner expects to return to a greater estate than he left with the steward.

6. While growth in total possessions is expected, at the same time the steward is expected to care for all the owner's interests generously during his absence. For example, all the owner's children shall be cared for abundantly before any consideration is given to generating a profit.

7. Upon the owner's return there will be an accounting of the possessions to determine if (A) the steward managed said possessions in faithfulness to the owner's wishes as stated in the *Book of Values;* (B) the steward adequately cared for the owner's children out of the proceeds of the operation.

The idea of stewardship became a natural illustration of the relationship the believer should have with his Heavenly Father regarding his possessions, material and otherwise. For instance:

1. God, the owner, has placed all possessions in our hands.

2. We are charged with the management.

3. Our daily decisions are to be made in light of God's best interests.

4. Our personal relationship with Christ and the Word of God is our guide in making these decisions.

5. We are expected to increase and develop our gifts and possessions.

6. This increase must never be at the expense of others.

In fact, God expects our care for others to rate higher as a priority than bringing an increase.

7. An accounting is coming when we will be judged on our faithfulness to care for the owner's property and gifts.

The concept of "stewardship" is a sound one to illustrate how we should view all possessions and gifts as from God. We are managers of *His* possessions. We are superintendents of *His* gifts. We are to be trustworthy in carrying out daily decisions in light of *His* values.

Money

The immediate application of the idea of stewardship concerns our money. The above principles suggest that God is the owner of all money. All funds I receive are merely entrusted to me to manage for Him. The idea of stewardship obliterates the notion of "a tenth is the Lord's." Stewardship says "Ten tenths are the Lord's!" Stewardship is making practical daily decisions as if all my funds are God's.

The question is no longer, "How much shall I give?" It becomes "How much shall I keep?" If all my income is truly God's, then His values must impact every purchase I make. As a true steward, I can never say, "I've paid my tithe. How I spend the rest is up to me." If I operate under the stewardship system, disturbing questions like these must come to my mind:

1. God expects me to care for myself, but when is "caring for myself" taken to excess?

2. Who are those "children of the owner" for whom He expects me to care – those in my church? my denomination? my country? the entire world?

3. Even though one person can't solve the whole world's problems, is that an excuse not to do my part?

4. In light of God's values, do I really need a new TV (car, dishwasher, or lawn mower)?

5. In what way will this purchase enhance God's work on earth?

6. If Jesus were in possession of this money, how would He spend it?

7. Am I comparing myself to others, rather than to the values in the Bible?

These questions are never fully answered for the sincere

believer. In fact, God expects us to wrestle continuously with them throughout our lives. This is uncomfortable to us. We would rather have a "cut-and-dried" set policy regarding money. For this reason, the concept of "pay your tithe and the rest is yours" is, by far, more commonly accepted than the idea of total stewardship.

Possessions

The idea of total stewardship extends beyond money to include all possessions. If I am a steward, then God is the owner of all I now hold. It is His pickup truck, His house, His dishwasher, and His stereo system. I am just the user of these items. He expects me to use them to further His work. Is this stretching things a bit? Can you really serve the Lord with your dishwasher, stereo system, house, or pickup truck? Read these stories.

Roberta is a busy schoolteacher. She is dedicated to her work and goes into the classroom early and often stays late. She considers her job a ministry and frequently takes opportunities to give her testimony in quiet ways to the other teachers and her elementary-age students. After school she spends much time grading papers, preparing for the next day, plus all her home duties – doing laundry, ironing, cleaning the house, washing dishes, reading stories to her two children, and helping her husband with his part-time small business. Beside all this, Roberta is the director of her church's midweek club program, and has been asked to take responsibility for the primary Sunday school class. She believes that having a dishwasher will save time each evening, to allow for this added responsibility. Is this purchase good stewardship?

Frank owns a sophisticated stereo system. This system is not just your average record player. It is one of those systems with dozens of knobs and buttons, and speakers as high as your chest. Frank, a single man, likes music. When he demonstrates his stereo system to his guests, the music reverberates through his small bungalow. The guests feel the music as well as hear it.

Recently, the church Frank attends has experienced a dramatic growth leap in the youth group – following construction of their new youth gym. Each Wednesday evening more than 75 teens meet for a weekly Bible study and share time. Frank helped out one evening. He was surprised to see the youth leader speaking without a P.A. system. The last straw came at the close of the meeting when the teens listened intently to a song correlated with the message of the evening. The record, done by a Christian musician, was played on the church's old phonograph. The sound came from tiny, inadequate speakers. Frank immediately offered to take his system to the gym each Wednesday evening for the youth leaders to use. Is Frank practicing stewardship of God's stereo?

Doris and Harry finally moved into their new house. They had saved for years and finally the opportunity came to buy a house with a large family room. They struggled a bit before the final decision, because they had always been very missions-minded. They had often dedicated any extra money to their "faith promise" giving. But, after prayerful consideration, they felt this was the right decision. Doris and Harry aren't the average homeowners. They are very particular. Some of the ladies assert that Doris dusts her furniture twice daily! Everyone knows from the way Harry keeps his lawn that this couple likes things kept perfectly neat.

Within three months after moving into their new house, Doris and Harry experienced the following: (A) The pastor's wife asked if the newly organized "Mothers of Preschoolers" group could meet each Monday in her home – with their preschoolers! (B) The youth group asked if they could have an outing at their house in the spring to play games on their lawn. (C) The midweek reminder asked for volunteers to entertain the visiting missionary coming for the missions convention. (D) Harry began consulting with his attorney regarding a will and the arrangements for the final distribution of his modest estate, including the house. In practicing the principles of good stewardship how might Doris and Harry decide in each case?

Dave, an outdoorsman, cuts firewood for a hobby. Last month he purchased a used pickup truck, promising the Lord it was available for His service at any time. Dave is not sure how all this would have gotten done before he bought his truck, but in one month he has been asked to haul railroad ties to use at the church parking lot, donate firewood for the church fellowship hall, "volunteer" the use of the truck for workday at camp, and pick up Mrs. Whitehall each Sunday morning until her lane dries up enough for a regular car to get her.

The truth from each of these situations is that with increased possessions come increased opportunities and obligations for service. If we practice total stewardship, God is the owner of all we have. As stewards we will use our material possessions to accomplish His will.

Time

The concept of stewardship does not end with money and possessions. It extends to intangibles like talents, spiritual gifts, and – perhaps most vital – time. If I am a faithful steward for God, I will spend my talents, my energy, and my time in light of His values. It may be far easier to tithe my income than to tithe my time. Faithful stewardship goes beyond financial tithing. All of my time is God's. All my talents and energies are God's. Since this is true, I must carefully measure where I put my time. If my gifts and abilities are God's and I am merely caring for them, for the time being, I should seriously examine (1) where I am investing the greatest part of my abilities, and (2) who is getting the most benefit from them.

Time is the universal equalizer. Everybody has the same amount each day. Even Jesus Christ had only 24 hours per day. His example illustrates that we should allot some time for rest, relaxation, going to wedding receptions, eating – even feasting! But he also invested His time in caring for the sick, outcast, diseased, and lonely. He spent large amounts of time in prayer, and a huge amount in teaching and training others.

Jesus expects us to do likewise, "redeeming the time," because of the importance of the task He has given us. Every hour we have on this earth is a gift from God. He wants us to be stewards of our time, investing it in activities which pay off for His work on earth.

Sanctification and Stewardship

Now back to the question we posed at the outset of this chapter: "Why should a book on holiness devote a chapter to the idea of stewardship?" What is the connection here?

The prerequisite for entire sanctification is my entire consecration. God does not completely cleanse and energize me until I make a total consecration of everything to God, including all my time, talents, energies, and money. Thus there is no choice, for a person walking the sanctified life, but to live a life of total stewardship. The notion "part for God, the rest for me," is absolutely foreign to a person who has totally consecrated his all to God. He or she has given all to God, and from that day of dedication forward, is making a commitment to live the life· of a faithful and trustworthy steward. As the Spirit leads him or her, daily decisions are based on, "what's best for God."This is the sanctified life.

BIBLE STUDY

1. What warnings and wrong values concerning money are found in each of the following scripture passages?
   a. Luke 12:15

   b. Luke 16:13-14, 19-31

   c. James 5:1-6

   d. Deuteronomy 8:17-18

2. What is the secret to being "wealthy" in Philippians 4:10-13?

3. Describe what happened among the early believers in Acts 4:32-35. Was this an "ideal for all to follow" or a "mistaken experiment"?

4. Money, possessions, and time are gifts from God to use. Based on the following scripture passages, how does God want me to spend these resources?
   a. 2 Corinthians 9:6-9

   b. 1 Timothy 5:8

   c. 1 John 3:16-19

   d. Romans 13:8

   e. Romans 13:4-7

   f. Romans 10:13-15

For Review and Discussion

1. What is the difference between the concepts of "tithing" or "giving to God" and the concept of "stewardship"?
2. Stewardship obviously relates to our money. To what else does it relate? How?
3. What does entire sanctification have to do with stewardship?
4. In caring for the needs of "the Owner's children," how far does God expect us to go? Are "His children" only believers – or does it include all men and women?
5. What is the relationship between wealth and contentment?

12

Sanctification and Security

What relationship does sanctification have to Christian security? Those who talk a lot about sanctification generally speak very little about security. Those who teach eternal security frequently speak little of sanctification. Is there any connection?

Relative Security

Since an entirely sanctified person can live above willful sin, some have wondered if this work of God in a person's heart makes him eternally secure. They reason that he never will sin again so he will never be lost. This is not true. There is no spiritual height or strength of grace from which it is not possible to fall and finally become lost. Sadly, there is much evidence around us illustrating spiritual "shipwreck."

This misunderstanding results from an inadequate comprehension of what God actually does in entire sanctification. Because of a new orientation of the heart, it is possible to live above willful sin. However, no intelligent proponent of entire sanctification would argue that sin becomes impossible. It is possible to not sin. But to commit sin is not impossible. Thus, if it is possible to rebel against the Lord and sin, it is possible to fall from grace and eventually be lost.

Security is a relative matter. For instance, I am sitting on a chair as I type these words. Unless I am overtaken by dizziness or other severe sickness, my chances of falling out of this chair are slight. However, if I stand on it, especially on the edge of the chair, I am more likely to fall – i.e., I am less secure. If the chair is placed on top of a table as I stand on it, my security is further jeopardized. Preposterous as it would be, if I were to stand on the chair while it is perched in the towering tree outside my window, I would be much less secure than sitting here in my office. Security is a relative thing – a person may be more or less secure, depending on where he is and what he is doing.

So it is with the security of believers. Our security is a relative matter. We may be more secure or less secure, depending on where we are and what we decide to do. There are two extremes here. On one hand there are those who insist on an unconditional security, no matter what. These argue that wherever I am, whatever I do, and regardless the extent of my rebellion, I continue to be a part of God's family. They say "once a son, always a son." On the other hand, some argue that it is not only possible, but even likely, that a believer will fall, resulting in a curious "eternal insecurity." Neither extreme is sound teaching.

As usual, truth is frequently found in the middle of the road. A believer should not ignore the possibility of becoming an easy target for the devil's devices and falling. Neither should he or she constantly fret about the likelihood of falling from grace and thus become a useless spiritual hypochondriac. There is a security for believers. It is not unconditional – unrelated to our own decisions about life. We may choose to walk precariously and place ourselves in danger of falling. But the chances of a believer unwittingly falling from grace are not so high that we need to live in crippling daily fear.

Sanctification and Backsliding

However, it would be evasive for this book not to address frankly the matter of backsliding as it relates to the sanctified life. We have seen that it is possible for a believer to fully consecrate his or her entire life to God, and then, in faith, receive God's cleansing and power. This is the event of entire sanctification. But the daily walk of the sanctified life must follow the event or experience. This daily walk is a repeated and continual walk of consecration and faith. It is "dying daily" by repeated consecration and habitual obedience to the Lord's clearly given directions.

What happens when a person walking in this way does not obey one of the promptings of the Spirit? For example, Beverly had lived a dedicated Christian life for years before she attended a ladies' retreat where the idea of entire sanctification was presented. She recognized that the one area of "holdout" for her was her unwillingness to witness for Christ to her unsaved friends at her work for the phone company. At the retreat she recognized the reason for her unwillingness to witness. She was more concerned about what her fellow employees thought of her than she was for the spread of the gospel. Some of her associates did not even know that she was a Christian.

At the closing service of the retreat Bev made a total dedication of herself to the Lord and, in faith, received His cleansing and power. She promised to make at least one attempt to share her faith every week from then on. New spiritual vigor came to Beverly during the next several months. Everyone seemed to notice "Bev's renewal." Then Christmas came. With the change of routine, and a vacation trip to her parents, she began to slack off on her commitment. The Lord would prompt her to say something to an unsaved associate at work, and she would willfully resist the idea until the opportunity passed.

Within a few weeks her newly begun habit of a daily time alone with God became less meaningful. Finally whole weeks went by without a day of Bible reading and prayer. Church services became dry and uninteresting to her. She noticed that her old habit of criticizing certain people at church was beginning to return. By Easter Beverly had to admit that the power she once knew was gone. She still felt she was a believer, but the zest and thrill she associated with the "sanctified life" was gone. She was sliding back, and she knew it.

What will happen to Beverly? Where will she go from here? There are three possibilities:

First, she might continue her slide into further disobedience. Refusing to witness when the Lord prompted had been followed by a drying up of personal devotions, which was soon followed by the return her critical spirit. These three areas of resistance to the Lord will be followed by others. Unless

Bev stops the slide, she may continue on back toward her old life. This will lead her into outright rebellion against God, and eventual lostness. Bev, who had tasted of the sweet life of total consecration, could actually even lose her membership in God's family if she continues her slide away from God.

Second, and perhaps more likely, Beverly may settle into a state of spiritual lukewarmness, going through the motions at church, but not experiencing the vitality of total surrender. Any person who has seriously interviewed today's church members would attest to the fact that many in our churches today fall into this second category. They once tasted of the life of total commitment for a period, then they began taking things off the altar of total consecration. Now they live on a plateau of lukewarmness.

Third, Beverly may respond to her realization that she is sliding back with the biblical response to disobedience – repentance. She may confess she has lost power, and recommit her all to Jesus, receiving His cleansing and power again. As we shall discuss in the next chapter, the sanctified life is maintained the same way it is obtained – by consecration and faith. This is a daily matter, and the life is maintained to the extent to which there is continual daily consecration and a sustained faith.

A sanctified believer can backslide through negligence, and head back toward the old life. If not checked, this backsliding may result in a life of lukewarmness and discontentedness, or eventual outright rebellion and loss of grace. A believer, no matter what his state of grace or growth, must consider any sliding back to be a serious matter. The trend of our lives tells us where we will be in the future. If that trend is backwards, trouble lies ahead. Backsliding must always be taken with utmost seriousness.

Sanctification and Security

While backsliding at any stage of growth must always be considered a present danger, we must on the other hand avoid becoming insecure. Our paranoia about security may keep us from doing anything constructive while we constantly check the state of our spiritual lives as if we expect to be falling from grace at any moment. Such negative expectations can become self-fulfilling prophecies.

Entire sanctification does relate to security. As we have

seen, security is a relative thing – a person may be more secure or less secure. This likelihood of falling is dependent on us – on the decisions we make. A person living the sanctified life is one who has totally surrendered to the Lord as the Master of his or her life. Jesus is the Boss. This total consecration means that the individual has firmly set the pattern that all future decisions will be in accordance with the will of Jesus Christ. All the time he or she is saying to God, "Not my will, but Thine." When decisions and promptings come in the future, the question will not be, "Do others do it?" or "Do I feel like doing it?" The only question is, Does the Lord want me to do this? The entirely sanctified person is totally committed to permanent obedience to God's will.

The relationship to security is clear. A person who constantly lives in obedience to God is totally secure as long as he continues to walk in obedience. This is a relative security. Security is relative to obedience.

The question relating to the person living the sanctified life is, "Will the entirely sanctified person be more likely to obey Christ?" The answer to this is an unequivocal "Yes!" Thus, the entirely sanctified person can be said to be more secure. He is not unconditionally secure; but as long as he walks in obedience, there need be no fear of falling.

God is not seeking an opportunity to "bounce" believers out of His family. Like a Father, He tenderly encourages, corrects, and chastens His children. If our lives are heading in the wrong direction, He nudges, rebukes, and delivers sometimes painful discipline in an attempt to awaken us and straighten us out. If we "despise" or rebel against this chastening and walk out of His home in rebellion, it is then we forfeit the grace He so freely gave to us.

The notion is false that a believer is unconditionally secure, no matter what he or she does. Yet, believers do have a conditional security which provides an assurance and certainty. God's work may be pursued with vigor and enthusiasm when perfect obedience reigns. There is little need for repeated introspection concerning our salvation if we are living in daily obedience to Christ. The crux of the entire matter is, "Am I obeying all known leadings of the Lord?" If I am, there is no need to worry about security. If I am not, then I should worry about the level of my obedience, not security. Security is not the central issue – it is obedience.

BIBLE STUDY

1. Each of these scripture passages illustrates the conditional security a believer has. Notice how frequently conditional words like "if" are used. Select several of the following scripture passages. From each scripture, respond to the question: "What will make (or keep) the believer secure?"
   a. Matthew 24:11-13
   b. Matthew 18:21-35
   c. Luke 8:11-15
   d. John 6:66-71
   e. John 8:31,32
   f. John 15:1-6
   g. Acts 11:21-23
   h. I Corinthians 15:1,2
   i. I Timothy 4:15,16
   j. I Timothy 5:14-15
   k. Hebrews 2:1-3
   l. Hebrews 6:4-9
   m. Hebrews 10:23-29

For Review and Discussion

1. Describe the three ideas of security – unconditional security, constant insecurity, and relative security.
2. Upon what is the believer's security dependent?
3. Is it possible for an entirely sanctified person to slide back but not all the way to being lost? In other words, could a sanctified believer revert to the life lived before entire sanctification but still be a Christian?
4. While an entirely sanctified person is not unconditionally secure, is he or she "more" secure?
5. What advice would you give to an entirely sanctified person to help them keep from sliding back?

13

Continual Cleansing

We who speak much about sanctification sometimes appear to emphasize the event of entire sanctification more than the life following this event. This is unfortunate; for all proponents of this work of God would hasten to affirm that the sanctified life is paramount to them. Of course, the life must have an initiation, thus the emphasis on being cleansed at one time. But the *continual* life of holiness is the central issue in all we have discussed.

The relationship of the wedding to married life is a parallel example. The wedding is the initiation of married life. It is a significant occasion, to be remembered throughout a person's entire life. But if a bride or groom expects to continually live in a wedding-day atmosphere, they will soon be disappointed. Marriage is life lived out in light of the wedding-day commitment.

This is equally true with sanctification. The event of sanctification may be remembered, all through a person's life, as the significant initiation it is. Yet, the continuous sanctified life, lived in light of that initial consecration, is of greater importance. The life does not come without the initiation; therefore, the one-time event is vital. But, if there is no life of holiness following that event, the event or "experience" is useless.

Entire sanctification must not be viewed as something done

"way back then," but as a life here-and-now – in the trenches of life. It is not a static life – you have arrived and are merely sitting around waiting to be taken to heaven. It is a life of active service to the Lord. Holiness is not final achievement, allowing a person to rest in their completeness. It is expandable. Further spiritual growth is the inevitable result. While the entirely sanctified person possesses love, compassion, joy, peacefulness, humility, and patience of the same quality as Jesus, the quantity of them is expandable.

The life of holiness is a daily walk with Christ. It is maintained by a continuous faith and consecration, which results in a continual cleansing by the Lord, our Partner in this journey.

A sanctified person is not exempt from the battles of life – never to be tempted again. The life of holiness is not without difficulties, struggles, temptations, and even defeats. The difference is that these foes are encountered with a firm settledness of will – "Not my will, but Yours be done."

Spiritual Dryness

Why in the world would a book on sanctification deal with the topic, "spiritual dryness"? Doesn't the Lord eliminate any possibility of dryness in the life of anyone who is entirely sanctified? Isn't the life of holiness one of constant bubbling and joy in one's soul? Could a sanctified person remain sanctified through a time when the enthusiasm, excitement,and thrill of growing in grace and serving Jesus evaporates?

To say the possibilities of spiritual dryness are gone for the sanctified would be untrue. Almost every person testifying to sanctification will honestly admit that there are times when God seems further away, daily study of the Word seems insipid, and church services leave the individual unmoved and bored. What has happened? Is the work of sanctification lost?

Such spiritual dryness results from several causes. Disobedience could be one cause. It is possible that God is urging the believer to move forward to a new area – say, being more generous in giving to God's work – and that he or she is resisting the idea. This resistance to moving forward will promptly dry up the soul of a sanctified believer. The sanctified life prospers in proportion to our obedience to His known leadings. Any resistance or foot-dragging will divert our lives onto a plateau of spiritual dryness from which the only return is repentance and renewed commitment.

However, resistance to the Lord's will is not the only cause of spiritual dryness. Many sincere believers have cast away their faith that the Lord had sanctified them fully when they hit the first dry plain in their Christian walk. Assuming that the sanctified life is one of continual joy and celebration, they figured that when things got difficult they had lost it all. So they gave up.

A great season of temptation can bring on a period of spiritual dryness. We can experience an assault from the tempter with such vengeance, and for so long a season, that our wrestling against evil leaves us spiritually wrung out. We have little joy or excitement about anything.

Another cause is "spiritual burnout." Christian workers are especially prone to this malady. It is possible to be so involved in church work, camps, retreats, evangelistic teams, counseling, and a million other spiritual activities that spiritual exhaustion results.

Physical burnout is another cause of spiritual dryness. A sanctified mother of three, with low iron, who is holding down a full-time job, carrying several responsibilities at church, and sleeping five hours per night will naturally be tired and bored in church services. Her heart will not leap at the idea of giving another night of her week to go soul-winning. Is she still sanctified? Yes. Likely she does not need to go to the altar as much as she needs to go to bed! Physical exhaustion can produce spiritual dryness.

The life of holiness is not based upon feelings. To be sure, a life of total submission has feelings associated with it. But reliance on feelings will bring discouragement. What we call "spiritual dryness" can sometimes come as a natural cycle of life. If it has been a general pattern of your life to be somewhat "blue" on Mondays, entire sanctification will not necessarily make your Mondays bright and exciting. One man was troubled because every spring he became discontented, preoccupied, and yearned to quit his job. Only after reflection did he discover that during the first eleven years of his married life he had moved home first from school, then to a summer job or elsewhere every single spring. His uneasiness was a result of this natural "cycle of life." Entire sanctification did not change his urge to do something different in the springtime.

It is important to determine the cause of spiritual dryness in the sanctified believer's life. If it is caused by willful resistance to the Lord, repentance is the only cure. But, if it is caused by physical or spiritual burnout, an assault of the tempter, or a natural cycle of life, we should be careful to recognize the reason for our "dryness" and not cast away our faith.

Continual Faith

The faith by which we obtain the work of entire sanctification is not merely a one-time exercise. It is a continual daily faith. To receive entire sanctification I must come to the point of saying, "I believe You are cleansing me – the work is done and I claim it by faith." To continue in this life the same kind of faith is necessary. For example, "I am continuing in this life today and I believe You continue to cleanse me."

Once doubt sets in, the life begins to slip away. As long as I believe it is possible to live without willful sin, the possibility of full obedience to the Lord is there. Once I begin to doubt the possibility, my life will follow my doubts. Continuous faith to maintain the sanctified life is as much a necessity as initial faith is for obtaining it.

Continual Consecration

To receive the cleansing and power connected with entire sanctification, total consecration is required. Likewise, to continue in this life, a continual consecration is necessary. At the event of our sanctification we settled the question of who will be the Lord of our life. As each of us continues to walk with Him, new areas will arise where continued consecration is required in light of the earlier one-time submission of our will to God.

These diagrams may help us to understand this process of "walking in the light":

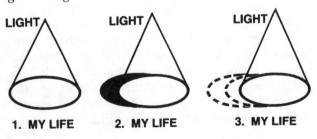

1. MY LIFE   2. MY LIFE   3. MY LIFE

At the initial event of our entire sanctification we consecrate all to God – our entire future, time, talent, money, reputation – everything. There are often one or two specific areas of holdout which focus on the question of who will be boss. However, when these are surrendered to the Lord, He is free to do His work of entire sanctification.

1. Usually there follows a period of joy and excitement as the sanctified believer now walks in full obedience to everything he or she clearly recognizes as God's will. It can be said that the believer's *life* is in harmony with all his known *light* from God.

2. But the sanctified life is not static. There is growth and expansion. How does this occur? God moves His light! In the midst of our living in total submission to all the past leadings of God, He leads again. He moves His light forward. Now two crescents appear – one, an area of my life outside of God's light. These are things He leads me to put off. They are not sin in themselves (yet, they may become sin if I refuse to lay them aside). Usually they are things of "second best" nature – items or practices not sinful, but nevertheless they are weights which slow me down in serving the Lord.

Some call these "convictions" – meaning that God has convinced them that certain things are better left beside the path if the race is to be run effectively. Obviously, these are very personal and can never be applied to others. When God moves His light forward, He often prompts us to lay aside particular things to make us more effective in serving Him. In this way the sanctified person experiences "conviction."

The second crescent includes new tasks and habits the Lord leads the believer to "put on." Perhaps the Lord convicts the sanctified believer to begin a weekly habit of soul-winning, or double tithing, or doing deeds of mercy for the poor. Again, this conviction is quite personal and cannot be generalized. And again, if the sanctified believer rebels against the Lord's guidance, sin will result.

3. The sanctified believer has settled the question – he or she will obey the Master whatever the cost. The natural result of this process of continual sanctification will be a stepping forward into the full brightness of God's revealed light. Now the believer's *life* again corresponds with all revealed *light*. The sanctified believer rejoices as he or she can say his life

is in full submission to the Lord in all areas where God's will is known.

This is the continuous walk of holiness. It is "walking in the light!" It is the natural expanding process of becoming more like Jesus. At the moment of entire consecration the issue was settled – my will was and is submitted completely to Jesus. Yet, there will be multitudes of challenging situations in my sanctified life that will provide opportunities for me to reaffirm that initial commitment. Making Him Lord of my life in one moment of consecration must be followed by keeping Him Lord of my life. This is done in subsequent times of reaffirmation.

Thus, the sanctified life, most simply put, is the obedient life. It is life lived out in light of a one-time commitment that Christ will be the absolute Lord of our lives from that day forward. It is the submissive life. It is a life where Jesus Christ is the daily leader, and we faithfully follow all of His promptings daily. It is a life of continuous growth and expansion as we obediently walk in the newly revealed light.

Where is this light headed? Why does He bring "new light" to us in this walk? Because He is constantly at work in us, conforming us into an image of His perfect Son. His light leads us closer toward Christlikeness. And we know that, if we are fully obedient to His leadings, we will one day be like Him and we shall see Him face to face. Until then, to the extent to which we are obedient, He is transforming us from "glory into glory," and we cannot even imagine what He intends to develop in us in the future. But that need not matter. Our task is to obey. Thus, the life of holiness – obedience.

Continual Cleansing

As we walk in this kind of obedience, His blood cleanses us. From what? Weren't we cleansed once and for all?

Christ's blood is a continued necessity for our daily walk. We will never reach a state of life when Christ's blood will no longer be needed. His blood continually cleanses the obedient believer as he or she walks in the light. We cannot receive a once-for-all cleansing and then go our merry way in self-reliance. We must rely daily on the blood of Christ for continual cleansing.

We need His blood to cleanse us from the thousands of

times we unknowingly fall short of His perfect standard. We need Christ's blood to continually cleanse us of every thought, attitude, word, or deed which does not edify and encourage. We need Christ's blood to cleanse us from the daily accumulation of "dust" we gather by traveling the roads of this world. We need the merit of Christ's blood to supply us with the daily cleansing required to maintain a life of holiness. This life is not self-maintained. It is maintained only as I am in a love relationship with Jesus Christ. Holiness is living as Jesus Christ lived. Holiness is walking in step with Jesus. If I am to be holy, it will only be in relationship with Jesus Christ.

Mildred Wynkoop illustrates this continued cleansing by asking readers to imagine themselves as suffering from defective kidneys. There is no hope in yourself – your blood supply is self-polluting. The only hope lies outside – if you can be attached periodically to a machine which will cleanse your blood. But suppose there was a way in which you could be attached to a healthy friend so that his kidneys could cleanse your polluted blood. Suppose that this friend was willing to be connected to you. So long as you were connected to this friend, and walking step by step with Him, your friend would insure a continuing perfection of your blood supply. An entire life-style would be established to maintain this moment-by-moment cleansing.

This is what holiness is all about. It is being connected to Christ in a daily obedient walk of submission. It is walking where He leads. It is relying on Christ, and Him alone, for cleansing. The life commences with a once-for-all yielding of ourselves to His will. And it continues as we are connected to Jesus Christ and walk in daily submission to His leadings.

Holiness is Christlikeness. Christlikeness is not reserved for a select few older saints or ministers. It is for every believer. Holiness is for ordinary people.

BIBLE STUDY

1. According to 1 John 1:5-7, on what is the continuous purification dependent?

2. Read Galatians 5:22-25. How do we "keep in step;" with the Spirit?

3. Read John 10:27. What relationship should we have to Christ as we follow His continued leadings?

4. Read John 15:5. What is the secret of the believer's continued vitality?

5. What is the specific request found in 1 Thessalonians 4:1?

For Review and Discussion
1. What parallel does this chapter make between the wedding/married life and entire sanctification/living the sanctified life?
2. What are some causes of spiritual dryness which even the entirely sanctified believer may experience?
3. Entire sanctification is obtained through consecration and faith. How is this life maintained?
4. In what area is God "moving His Light forward" for you?
5. For what does the entirely sanctified person need "continual cleansing"?

AFTERWORD

If you are interested in this total cleansing, yet you are not sure you have received this work of God, what should you do? You should "keep on keeping on." Holiness is not a message designed to bludgeon honest believers into despair by telling them they are defective. It is a message of hope, encouragement, and possibility. It marches into your life saying, "You can do it. You can be Christlike, with God's help."

Sometimes this message of optimism has the reverse effect on sincere Christians. The idea of perfect love for God and others may seem so distant a possibility to you that you are tempted to give up in despair, or say the whole teaching must be false.

Don't respond either in despair or in doubt. If you are sincerely interested in the whole matter of becoming fully Christlike, keep seeking! How?

(1) STUDY. Keep reading books, pamphlets, testimonies, magazine articles, and especially God's Word. Ask people, who live exemplary lives, about holiness. Ask God, "If this is really true, show me clearly in Your Word." No one is asking you to accept a dogma without thinking. Use your own mind. Study the matter thoroughly, so that you might become convinced of truth.

(2) PURSUE HOLINESS. Even if you are unclear about entire sanctification, you certainly would not deny God's progressive sanctification in your life right now. Undoubtedly you would agree that it is God's goal to change His children into the image of His own Son – in word, thought, and action. So, follow hard after holiness. Pursue it with single-minded intensity. Become a "seeker." Actively crucify the deeds of the flesh. Methodically put on thoughts, words, and actions of righteousness. If you seek holiness, you will find it. If you hunger and thirst for righteousness, you will be filled.

(3) CONTINUALLY CONSECRATE YOURSELF. God wants all of you – all of your thoughts, words, actions, talents, habits, time, possessions, every part of you. What areas in your life are not now under the Lordship of Jesus Christ? Practice continually bringing each of these under His full authority.

Hold nothing back. As He prompts you to yield a new area to Him, do so immediately, joyfully, and without resistance. Allow the Holy Spirit to fill every corner of your entire life. Resist Him at no point. Give Him your all.

(4) RECEIVE THIS WORK BY FAITH. Your study, pursuit of holiness, and continual consecration will invariably lead you to a point of decision. The moment the Holy Spirit convinces you that He wishes to completely cleanse and empower you, surrender completely to Him. Reach out in faith and receive entire sanctification. Begin living the sanctified life. How is it that you were converted? All your self-adjustment wouldn't save you. You finally had to reach out in faith and say, "Save me now."

So it is that you can say, "Fill me now," and God's sanctifying work will be done. How many times have you said. "Be gone!" to anger, jealousy, hatred, pride, impure thoughts, unholy habits, and the like. Yet, they stay on. These spirits are stronger than you are. The Holy Spirit, however, is The Strong Man. It is He alone who can drive these inclinations from the temple of your heart. The fullness of the Holy Spirit drives out everything contrary to His Spirit, just as when the sun rises the darkness flees. Let the Son rise in your heart!